D1236984

MODERN TEACHING
Edited by P. W. Musgrave

TELEVISION IN EDUCATION

TELEVISION IN EDUCATION

Roderick MacLean

METHUEN EDUCATIONAL LTD
11 New Fetter Lane · London EC4

First published 1968 by Methuen Educational Ltd
© 1968 by Roderick MacLean
Printed in Great Britain by
Butler and Tanner Ltd
Frome and London

This title is available in both hard bound and paperback editions. The paperback edition is sold subject to the condition that it shall not, by way of trade or otherwise, be lent, re-sold, hired out, or otherwise circulated without the publisher's prior consent, in any form of binding or cover other than that in which it is published and without a similar condition including this condition being imposed on the subsequent purchaser.

Distributed in the U.S.A.
by Barnes & Noble Inc.

Contents

List of Illustrations

Preface

This is a dangerous time at which to offer a book that deals with educational television in Britain: dangerous because it is a field in which, after a slow start, there are now so many developments. A year or two can change the picture quite substantially, and such forecast as one ventures may so rapidly be proved inaccurate. But survey rather than forecast is the main purpose of this study.

The recent proliferation of closed circuit systems has sometimes been accompanied by an element of confusion as to the exact role they are designed to play: a confusion which – though it may seldom have existed in the minds of those educationists directly concerned – has often afflicted their colleagues even more than the layman who in the long run pays for broadcasting and closed circuit systems alike. As one who has been involved in both uses of the medium, I have tried to establish the responsibilities and the areas of activity that most appropriately belong to each: and the more clearly one recognizes the proper differences between broadcasting and closed circuit, the more convinced one becomes that their functions can – and must – be developed on a complementary rather than a competitive basis.

My approach to the subject has been frankly insular. Those of us immediately engaged in educational television are naturally aware of all the work that has already been done in the United States; and we are glad to learn from it, though many of the comparisons and the statistics that America offers us are not strictly relevant to our own circumstances. This is an account of current developments here in Britain, of things which – though often on a small scale – are actually happening.

Which brings me to one final point. There is something about the word 'television' that encourages the most competitive and exaggerated claims. Every new educational studio is 'the first of its kind'; every closed circuit system 'the biggest in Western Europe'; television itself, of course, is going to 'revolutionize educational techniques.' Let us keep things in proportion. It would be a pity if we were so to over-sell the possibilities as to foster our own disillusionment.

R. C. M.

Acknowledgements

Chapter 4 is adapted from four articles which appeared in *The Times Educational Supplement* during December 1966 and January 1967, and the author and publishers are grateful to the original publishers for permission to reproduce this material. They also wish to thank Photocraft of Dunfermline for permission to reproduce the illustration facing p. 23 (bottom), and The Marconi Company Limited for that facing p. 87 (bottom).

CHAPTER ONE

Towards a Definition

It is no bad thing, whatever the subject of one's study, to start off by defining terms. So you might reasonably expect to discover, in these opening lines, an answer to the question – What is television? But sometimes – and this is a case in point – the real task is not so much to introduce a subject with which we are all acquainted, as to strip off the layers of prejudice and woolly thinking that have gathered around it. Television's history is short: as we know it in Britain, it is younger than most of the people who are likely to read this book. Yet in the course of that short history a number of historical and organizational accidents have contributed towards the hardening of ideas about television which could all too easily work against its most productive use in the field of education.

Consider two of these accidents. First, that for a quarter of a century television has grown up primarily as a vehicle for entertainment and journalism. Second, that the television which reaches us in our homes – whether it be news, or a religious service, or music hall, or a schools broadcast – is all part of an output subject to centralized control: no longer monopolistic in Britain, but largely centralized. Now these two accidents have combined to produce two mistakenly rigid ways of thinking about television, both of which are likely to prove pitfalls for the educator who is toying with its possibilities.

Television in Education

Because television's news and light entertainment and sport and all the rest of it reach us through one single viewing-box, we fall too readily into the habit of speaking about television as 'a medium' – a colloquially convenient description which can soon obscure the fact that television in reality effects a merely technical conjunction of many quite different media. Equally, because entertainment and journalism have bulked so large in television's output, and because broadcast programmes are seen by so many people, we fall into the trap of describing television invariably as 'a mass medium'. This it often is, both in terms of technique and in terms of the sheer numbers reached: but to speak of it constantly as a mass medium is to overlook the fact that many of its most successful uses, not least some of its educational applications, are successful simply because television can achieve a one-to-one relationship which is the very reverse of mass medium techniques.

Look for a moment at the implications of our calling television a medium – speaking, that is, as if it were one single medium. We rightly describe any form of human communication as a medium when it exerts some recognizable and fairly constant modifying and adapting effect upon the material with which it deals. Drama – to take one obvious example – over-simplifies, heightens, and therefore clarifies the personal relationships which it examines: when we speak of theatre as a medium, we are referring to this recognizable function of underlining the essentials by over-simplifying and 'dramatizing' a human situation. Or consider the press: by its selection of items, its emphasis on one aspect rather than another, and by its style of presentation, a newspaper can direct and control the awareness of its readers and foster particular views or attitudes. These techniques are recognizable, and in exercising them journalists are using the press as a medium of communication. To take another quite different example, church worship can be described as a medium because, being a corporate and shared activity, it adds a new dimension and modifies individual religious experience in a quite characteristic way. All these

2

techniques and many more television will use from time to time and in different items; but the medium, the adapting influence, does or should differ from programme to programme. If television were itself a single medium, it would impose the same stamp on everything it transmitted, and have the same adapting influence on everything from a boxing match to a documentary.

Perhaps indeed this has begun to happen. Perhaps we do see too many examples of, say, the current affairs programme in which a producer has borrowed techniques and imposed interpretations that belong legitimately to his colleague in the drama department. Sometimes, too, one sees what is essentially a straightforward teaching programme unbecomingly tricked out in what is almost certainly a misguided attempt to give it superficial appeal. In both cases we are witnessing the results of a belief that television is all of one kind, that achieving the 'televisual' is the primary aim – in short, that television constitutes one medium.

What, you may ask, is the relevance of all this to educational television? Simply that one cannot blame the more cautious and conventional educators who, conditioned into believing that all television is one and the same thing, choose as their yardstick the less desirable aspects of their own viewing experience, and argue that the treatment of a subject by television necessarily means popularized and superficial treatment. If we are to think only in terms of broadcasting to a non-captive and sometimes almost accidental audience, this may well be the case: on these terms we must accept relative superficiality as a necessary shortcoming; but the superficiality does not lie in the nature of television itself, it should be attributed instead to the nature of the non-captive audience and its predictable behaviour. Television, when it is fully adapted to the educational context, is capable of all the depth and all the insight that ever went into an act of classroom teaching. But this *full* adaptation implies two conditions that are not always recognized in the discussion of educational television – first, that the audience must be as

3

committed as it would be in a conventional classroom situation; and second, that the television treatment must not flirtatiously compete with the quite different entertainment type of television.

There is no point in glossing over the fact that these two conditions do, at this point in time, demand quite strict self-discipline on the part of students and teachers alike. In its short lifetime, television has become so firmly associated with attitudes of relaxation and passivity that there is a real danger of a student's expecting anything shown on television monitors to be a soft option to conventional teaching. For the teacher, on the other hand, the danger is that he may be tempted into meeting the student's expectation halfway: that he may – without being really conscious of it – carry over into his television teaching some of the techniques (call them gimmicks, if you will) which have become associated with television merely because it has until now usually meant entertainment.

One apparently trivial example may make the point. Very few of us, as lecturers or teachers, have made a practice of entering our classrooms to the strains of signature music. If we did, our students' reactions would probably force us to give the deepest consideration to our precise choice of music, so that it could not be subject to inappropriate interpretation. Yet one finds quite often that, when closed circuit television is used for the routine business of lecturing, signature music tops and tails the performance as a matter of course. Is this of any great importance one way or another? No, except that on the one hand it subtly suggests to the student those same conditions of relaxation and passivity that are associated with domestic entertainment; and, on the other, it may indicate that the teacher has uncritically carried over to this new context some other irrelevant trimmings of what is really quite a different medium.

Television, one must reiterate, is not a single medium. It can represent the lightest of light entertainment; it can compete with the qualities of serious journalism; it can also – fully

4

adapted – offer a channel for the most effective of straight teaching. But here the essential point is its adaptation to the educational context. If television teaching is to confound the perfectly reasonable fears that it will prove superficial, it can do so only by being consciously and positively different from a great deal of broadcast television as we know it. To say this implies no criticism of broadcast television as such: it is simply a question of recognizing that a broadcasting organization by its very nature must always have at least two audiences in mind – a relatively committed audience, and a much larger chance audience, for both of which it has a responsibility to cater. It is to be expected, therefore, that only within closed circuit systems – where a wholly committed audience can be taken for granted – are we likely to see television's fullest adaptation to the purposes of direct teaching.

See how easily confusion emerges in the discussion of television, particularly if the questions at issue are those of its educational application. One begins an argument by using the word, as we all do, to mean broadcast television. We cite evidence based on our experience as broadcasters or as home viewers. Then in a sentence we slip in some reference that can only apply to closed circuit television – a world that is often as different from broadcasting as the textbook is from the popular magazine. And then, still using the same words (for we are desperately short of adequate vocabulary in these developing years), we find ourselves back on the broadcast side of the argument again and making heavy weather of it. In later chapters it will be appropriate to look at broadcast and closed circuit television quite separately, but while we are still speaking ambiguously of both varieties, let us take a look at the second cliché definition which is regularly applied, with the most confusing results.

Rightly or wrongly, we will of course continue to speak of television as 'a medium'. It is too convenient a description to be dropped, however strong the arguments are against it. One must hope, however, that we shall look more critically at our habit of speaking about it as though it were necessarily and always a 'mass medium'. A great deal of loose thinking about the educational use of television has been based upon just this description. That it can and does constitute a very influential method of mass communication is beyond dispute; but to remain from hour to hour an active means of mass communication, its transmissions must have mass appeal: otherwise a million switches up and down the country will rapidly belie our definition. Herein lies the fallacy to which the educator is sometimes all too ready a victim – the belief that television in itself offers the prospect of revolutionary advances in the size of our willing audience. Such enthusiasm springs from the naïve belief – based on experience of the domestic receiver – that anything, by virtue of being televised, acquires a wider appeal. This is patent nonsense, but a surprising number of people believe it. The mere interposition of a camera adds no magic quality to the material it surveys. If what goes into the camera has mass appeal, then the chances are that some element of that appeal will reach the receiver. If the material offered to the camera is dull and ineffective, then by the time it reaches the viewer these faults will have multiplied rather than disappeared. Television of itself will not revolutionize the style and quality of our education; nor will a technically efficient method of distribution necessarily provide us with a willing mass audience.

This is the fundamental distinction, blurred by our loose use of the expression 'mass medium' – that television, if we are thinking of the nation-wide networks, does offer a distribution system of quite vast proportions; but that it only becomes a mass medium in any real sense of that term when the material transmitted is of such a nature, or is so manipulated, that it will catch and hold a mass audience. We should not ignore or despise the idea of using television for merely distribution purposes – a point to which we shall return when we are considering television in Adult Education. But equally we must not imagine that the use of a potentially vast distribution system automatically confers the virtues or implies the vices of mass medium techniques.

When we turn to closed circuit systems, on the other hand, we are usually dealing with conditions in which we would never previously have considered ourselves to be involved in mass communications at all. Most teachers would pride themselves on communicating with their pupils in as individual and personal a way as circumstances permit. The paradox is that we should so often hear the educational uses of television justified on the basis of its use in a mass medium setting.

Because we fail to differentiate clearly enough the separate and very various uses of television, because we are inclined to associate with any one of its applications the conclusions that spring from its use in a quite different context, because in short we use the single word 'television' indiscriminately to describe activities that would be given a dozen different names if they were in print – because of all that, the real stumbling block in the early stages of educational television is that the word itself conjures up a whole host of loosely connected associations, many of them irrelevant to the educational aim, most of them derived wholly from the domestic receiver in the sitting-room at home. Thus a primary school teacher, conscious that her pupils are better informed on world affairs than she was at their age, reasonably links this observation with the knowledge that her pupils watch some of the more responsible current affairs programmes: and she attributes this widening of their horizons to 'television'. Your academic politician or economist, on the other hand, may deplore the compression and simplification that such programmes often impose on complex ideas; and he will accuse 'television' of being glib and superficial. Yet another observer, equally responsible in his own field of youth work, will have reason to be aware that teenage delinquency in his own area is on the increase: he too is likely to see 'television' as a contributory factor, but for him the word implies the highly coloured thriller or the realistic play. In the field of religion, again, television has offered a platform for discussion and debate rather than merely a channel for the relaying of public worship: so a critic will understandably complain that 'television' encourages doubt rather than conviction. Each offers relevant comment in his own field: each contributes to a total pattern of associations which is complex, often confused, and every part of which appears at times to contradict many of the others.

Small wonder, then, that there was sometimes a confusion of motives when universities and colleges and local authorities began seriously to think of using television. Small wonder that enthusiasts and critics alike drew on this confused wealth of associations for ammunition to justify or to confound the proposals. Journalism and entertainment had had a quarter of a century's head start in the use of television, and now television was in danger of being judged not as itself but as a suspect amalgam of the other two. If we are not to fall into this very trap of basing conclusions on largely irrelevant associations, we must draw a quite sharp distinction between two different approaches and intentions.

On the one hand we may have, on the broadcast channels, programmes which are in a broad and general sense educative in their intention, programmes designed for an audience which is – to begin with at any rate – completely uncommitted, programmes which translate into television terms every appropriate journalistic device for catching and holding the attention of a mass audience. After such a programme one is likely to have a new awareness of the subject dealt with; one will have gained, at least superficially, some new knowledge; because of home viewing conditions one will almost certainly retain a few *mis*-impressions of what was said; but one's experience of the programme alone could not justify a claim to have been studying the subject. All this adds up to television in the generally accepted sense; and if there are elements of superficiality and mis-impression, they are certainly no greater than those which characterize the feature articles of any newspaper or magazine. The end result, even though it does not constitute study, is on the side of information rather than of ignorance.

But set against that the quite different approach and intention of the educational institution. Here the commitment is to

8

teach directly, to study with some degree of concentration. Can the superficial television approach be harnessed to meet this need? The question is wrong, of course, because its very wording implies an unfavourable answer – yet that is how we often ask it. Either on a broadcast transmission or on a closed circuit system, television can be used in many ways for the most direct of direct teaching; but if we are to examine what its most effective contributions can be in this more strictly defined educational setting, we must begin by shedding all its stock associations. We must forget, so far as we can, how the issues have been clouded and sensationalized by 'Coronation Street' and 'Perry Mason' and 'The Avengers' and innumerable visits to the kitchen sink. For the moment, too, we must leave out of the reckoning the many excellent documentaries which are indisputably educative, but which fall outside the category of direct teaching; and we must ask ourselves the simple question:

'Supposing that television were, in this year of grace, a new invention: supposing that it had been presented first to us as educators, a brand new facility for use in teaching: what claims would we now be making for it?'

CHAPTER TWO

A Measure of Capacities

Basically, the capacities that television offers us are remarkably simple; and they are by no means as novel as we keep telling ourselves. They can be reduced to a fundamental four – the capacity to magnify what is observed; the capacity to relay or distribute vision instantaneously (and usually the related sound along with it); the capacity (by using videotape) to store visual material; and the capacity to assemble large amounts of hetero-geneous material into one coherent whole. And the surprising thing is this, that only one of these functions is new and peculiar to television – the capacity to distribute vision instantaneously. All the others we have already been able to achieve in a variety of ways – there is no lack of devices that will magnify as effec-tively as the television camera; film, if we take the trouble to use it, can operate as a means of both storing visual information and subsequently distributing it; sound radio and sound film are no strangers to us; and as for the assembling of heterogeneous material into a coherent teaching pattern, surely film can do this too?

All this is true. There are a great many things about television which only seem to be new. The real novelty of its value to us lies first in its adaptability as a means of distribution, and second in the fusion and permutation of the other capacities we have mentioned. Seldom are these in fact used singly; but for the sake of exposition it is simplest, if a little artificial, to separate the four factors and examine each by itself.

Look first, then, at the simplest of the four facilities offered – the capacity to magnify images and simultaneously distribute them. But what's wrong with the traditional magnifying devices? What's wrong, for example, with the microscope? Absolutely nothing: except, if we are to take the microscope as our example, that the owner of an untutored eye habitually lies about what he sees with it when he applies it to the eyepiece. The television camera takes the microscope, properly adjusted by a skilled demonstrator, adds its own degree of magnification to the image, and distributes it around the laboratory or the classroom on as many monitors as you need to as many students as are present. The number of students you can reach, of course, depends entirely on the extent of your distribution system. Does this amount to substituting second-hand experience for individual personal experience? Not at all: no one is suggesting that such a use of television will ever replace the student's own handling of materials and equipment – but there are many skills in the early stages of whose teaching it is important to know that the student really does see what he must see. In such cases, where in an ideal world we would be teaching groups of four or five at most, a simple use of television provides the solution for the teaching of groups a hundred times that size.

The use of the television camera along with the microscope is a particularly straightforward and striking example – where in the past only one pair of eyes could see at any one time, now a dozen or a hundred pairs can as easily follow the detail while it is pointed out by the teacher. However this is only one example of many teaching situations in which television's straightforward capacity for magnification can be brought to bear. To cite a few cases from university work – in pathology, television presents medical students with the magnified detail of human tissues while their characteristics are being discussed by the lecturer; a whole class of dental students can simultaneously study a

11

single cavity while their lecturer indicates treatment; in botany, plant dissections are seen in every detail while they are carried out by a demonstrator; in geology, minute and valuable fragments can be closely examined with the minimum of handling. And so the list goes on. Could film cope just as well? In purely visual terms, yes. In teaching terms, no: because television in such cases has the peculiar strength that it deals with what are obviously real-life here-and-now situations. The examples shown, the demonstrations offered, are not ideal textbook examples and therefore somehow remote: the situations are presented and dealt with by the normal teacher, and to their manifest reality is added the tremendous value of complete visibility.

So far we have cited examples drawn from university work; but of course there are just as many school situations to which this simple application of television applies. In school, as in university, the camera will offer something more than a front-seat view of chemistry and physics demonstrations, and in needlework, knitting, cookery, technical subjects – wherever there is a demand for the detailed demonstration of practical skills to more than a very few pupils at one time – the simplest of television installations may well be the answer; and at this level of provision the cost of television can be very moderate in relation to the advantages it offers.

Now it may seem that all this is a far cry from the television that is spoken of as a mass medium; and indeed it is, though for lack of other words we describe it by the same name. This is television used simply as a visual aid, often wholly within the classroom or laboratory. Nothing very exciting, certainly nothing revolutionary: nothing invoking any educational principle more profound than that it is better to see than not to see, better to see well and intelligibly than to depend on hearsay and imagination. In short, a perfectly respectable function of the sheer mechanics of television.

Next look at television's capacity to relay, to distribute the images observed, to carry the sound and vision of what is

12

happening at point A simultaneously and instantaneously to points X, Y and Z. In broadcasting, of course, the images are relayed or distributed to an infinite number of points: in closed circuit work, although the principle is the same, a relay may be designed to reach a very few remote points, or only one. Since wide distribution is so obvious and so familiar a characteristic of broadcast television, there is no need to dwell on it here; look instead at the advantages of relay as they affect the educational situation within a school or college. When is it an advantage to be in two places at one and the same time? – for that, essentially, is the benefit which television really offers you. It is possible, though perhaps a little glib, to answer by categories and say that television relay comes into its own whenever conditions at the point of transmission are too cramped, too hot, too dangerous, too inaccessible, too intimate to permit the presence of those whom you wish to teach. This list is incomplete, but it will do for a start.

Take the more mechanical situations to begin with. A class in computing science must be given some practical acquaintance with the computer, but cannot be accommodated in the computer room: so our cameras go there in their place and relay their account of the computer to the lecture theatre. Experiments in heat engineering, experiments involving radioactive substances – in these two cases again, television obviously comes into its own. But this is relay in the most mechanical of senses: there are instances in which it can enter much more subtly into the teaching situation. In the teaching of psychology or psychiatry, for example, there are frequently test and interview situations in which the subject's behaviour and performance may be substantially affected by the presence of a class of students. Experience shows that the same situations can be covered by television in the privacy of a small room and relayed, with better teaching effect, to students who are watching elsewhere. In the allied fields of medicine and surgery, the same television techniques are making it possible to reduce the number of occasions on which groups of students are actually taught at the bedside in the hospital ward; for here again the camera's output can reach larger groups of students and at the same time reduce the amount of intrusion on the patient and disturbance in the ward.

These are practical considerations of some importance, and would in themselves justify the use of television for relay; but there is good reason for believing that in such settings television adds a new dimension of its own to the quality of the teaching itself. This is true, too, when relay is used as a way of breaking down the rigid barriers which have sometimes grown up between theoretical teaching and practical experience, between lecturing and laboratory work. In a subject like chemistry, for example, where for good practical reasons a class will sometimes have to meet in the lecture room and sometimes in the laboratory, television can link the two so that theoretical exposition and practical demonstration can be directly related to each other.

Magnification we described as the mere use of the mechanics of television. The function of relay may be purely mechanical also; but the material relayed may range from straightforward magnification, through the coverage of a lecture for an overflow audience, to a highly complex programme. An equally wide range of possibilities is covered by television's third capacity – the capacity to store visual material for subsequent use. By this we mean, of course, that the output of our cameras can be recorded on videotape and played back (within certain technical limitations) wherever and as often as we need it. A videotape recorder, perhaps one ought to explain, records sound and vision in much the same way as the normal tape recorder stores sound. As with the sound recorder, so the videotape recorder (VTR for short) offers immediate playback once the recording has been made; and a video-recording can be wiped or erased just like a sound tape, so that a new recording can be made.

To add a videotape recorder to even a small television installation is to multiply its usefulness out of all proportion to the expense involved. The usefulness of its capacity to store visual material will be implicit in several later chapters, so it will suffice at this stage merely to enumerate a few examples. A complicated demonstration, involving detailed preparation and the setting-up of equipment, can be given once in front of the camera, recorded, and played back on numerous occasions to different classes or groups. The acquisition of some practical skill can be assisted by the recording and immediate playback for self-assessment of the pupil's own performance – at university level this has been successfully applied to skills as diverse as golfing, swimming and preaching. Recording makes it possible to bring back into the school or college material that is only available outside – an industrial process recorded in a local factory for study in the school; observation of school classroom behaviour recorded for analysis in the teacher training college; the compilation of medical case-histories in hospital wards and in patients' own homes for subsequent demonstration to medical students. The possibilities are as innumerable and as various as are the needs of the schools and colleges concerned.

We have looked separately at the capacity to magnify, to relay, and to record or store for later use. To do so is of course unrealistic, since in practice we are likely to be using at least two of these capacities at any one time. The image which we magnify is one which we also relay and perhaps distribute quite widely; the demonstration which we relay from laboratory to classroom is just as likely to be one which we also record for repeated use. As we said earlier, it is in the fusion and permutation of these capacities that we find the real value of television. The idea of fusion and permutation also enters largely into what we suggested as television's fourth claim on the attention of the teacher – the capacity to 'assemble'.

This is of course a shorthand expression and it means nothing without a word of explanation. Much of our teaching, whether it is at school or at university level, amounts to the propounding of arguments based upon evidence which we do not present, evidence which the pupil is asked simply to accept. This is not to be taken as a foolish and wholesale condemnation of teaching method; nor, of course, is it true of all our teaching. But most students, whatever their faculty, will recognize phrases

15

like – 'Once you're out teaching you'll discover . . .'; or 'When you're in practice you may come across . . .'; or 'If you were to try this out in the lab . . .'. All of them phrases designed to indicate the existence of evidence; but evidence elsewhere, not here. To produce the evidence in the conventional classroom surroundings would normally be impracticable and distracting. This is the situation in which television, with its capacity to assemble the evidence, really makes its quite distinctive contribution to teaching technique. The degree of sophistication with which we assemble the evidence will depend on the amount of equipment available and the ingenuity with which we operate it: but even a couple of simple cameras will make it possible to bring together photographic stills and slides, charts and animated captions, working models and perhaps even clips of film, in such a way that they fuse unobtrusively into one coherent whole. Presented as individual items, they might add up to distraction and clutter, and some might be barely visible. As television, they reach the classroom through the single uncluttered focus of attention which is the television monitor.

All this may sound grandiloquent: and naturally it must be related to the level of the television equipment that is available. But television studios are no longer the rare exception that they were only a few years ago; and when we make full use, in such a way as this, of the resources offered by even a modest studio, we are moving towards documentary – if we can borrow the most nearly appropriate word from broadcasting. In other contexts we may have been using merely the mechanics of television; here we are certainly beginning to use its intrinsic capacities to add a new dimension to our teaching.

It is one thing to describe what television can ideally do: it is quite another to forecast the ways in which the educational use of television will actually develop. Our description of the possibilities has so far been an account written very much from the television standpoint, as though we all *had* or *wanted* television and were merely wondering how best to employ it. In practice, however, that is scarcely the way in which things work. So far as closed circuit equipment is concerned, the great majority of us will find the money to acquire it only when there is seen to be a pressing educational need. So far as broadcast educational television is concerned, at both school and higher levels, there is currently a tendency to move away from the more general approach that used to be described as 'enrichment' towards more direct acts of teaching. But looking forward over the next few years, it seems reasonable to forecast that educational television (in both the broadcast and the closed circuit fields) will develop most vigorously and effectively where the peculiar capacities of television and the actual demands of education meet. If we are to enumerate the points at which these capacities and demands do meet, we shall to some extent be re-stating points that have already been made; we shall certainly be slipping – but consciously – into ambiguous references which may apply sometimes to broadcast and sometimes to closed circuit transmissions; but at least it will be an attempt to state the case primarily from the educator's point of view.

Television seems likely to establish itself wherever immediacy is of value as a factor in teaching – wherever the feeling of really being there, of really being involved, is going to add impact. This may be immediacy of time, or immediacy of place. Normal run of the mill broadcasting has nowadays accustomed us to an extravagant degree of stress on immediacy of time, so that it is becoming a commonplace to witness events while they are actually taking place a continent or an ocean away. For most teaching purposes, however, immediacy of time seems likely to remain relatively unimportant – we *can* watch an operation here in Britain while it is taking place in the United States, but our students would normally gain just as much advantage from seeing a recording of it next day or a film of it next week. True, in a field like modern studies the live transmission of, say, procedure in the House of Commons might have considerable value; but in practical terms – and still taking modern studies as our example – what television can effectively offer is the central

17

availability of expert commentators, capable of adding to the impact of such a subject by relating it to events of immediate topicality. However it is in offering immediacy of place that television will be most welcomed by the teacher; and to say this is simply to re-phrase what has already been said about relaying, recording and distributing. A whole range of items – the microscopic, the remote, the merely awkward – can be brought into the classroom to replace 'I have heard about it' with 'I have seen it'.

Then there is the type of study in which the provision, or the restoration, of context is a matter of importance. Here again television will prove its value. Take as a simple example the early stages of learning a foreign language. We all learn our own language in its context: we gradually associate words with the objects they represent because the people around us use the words in relation to those objects. Schoolroom learning of a language has often, and of necessity, been divorced from the context. Of recent years we have had many excellent examples in broadcast programmes of the way in which television can restore the context in language teaching. These broadcast programmes have normally been aimed at an adult audience; but since 1965 Glasgow's closed circuit system has been putting exactly the same principles into effect in the teaching of French to primary pupils. If languages provide a rather obvious example, there are many more – among them mathematics, science, geography. One is not suggesting that only television can perform this function; merely that it has a peculiar facility for performing it, and that this is likely to be one of the lines along which it will most fruitfully develop.

Next, one would suggest that television will have a contribution to make wherever the unconscious manipulation of attention is of value. Stating it thus baldly, one is liable to be accused of sinister intentions – echoes of subliminal suggestion and the like. But in fact one is merely presenting, from a slightly different standpoint, television's capacity to assemble a wide variety of evidence. Look at it this way. In the conventional classroom

18

situation, a pupil or student sits relatively immobile. Should there be any demonstration of a practical nature, he sees only one aspect of it. Take this simple situation and translate it into television terms. For a start, you will probably bring two or three cameras to bear on the demonstration – offering, in effect, several pairs of eyes; and by your choice of shots you will from moment to moment present your student with that aspect of the situation which is for the time being most significant. In that sense, you are manipulating his attention. But add now to that simple situation all the additional sources of information that may be available to you even in a small television installation – film, explanatory captions which can be superimposed, animations which can add force to a spoken argument. Add all these, and you have a situation in which the television teacher is first established on the monitor as the focus of attention, and is then replaced at his will by the material towards which he wants to direct attention. Because the monitor has been established as the single focus, references to the changing material need not be too didactically explicit. When this is well done – and we often see it done badly – the speaker and film and photographic stills and captions can all be presented almost without the viewer's awareness of the changes: his attention is focussed throughout on the developing theme. The unobtrusiveness of this manipulation depends on infinitely careful preparation, scripting and timing; but if these can be achieved, the result fully justifies the use of television as a teaching technique.

It would, however, be naïve to suppose that educational television will develop only where educational principle most justifies it. So one must allow for the probability that in practice it will develop in one form or another where administrative necessity demands that it should. Thus in the university world we can expect that television will be used increasingly to cope with the problem of a growing student population. This it will do, of course, in a variety of ways. The pre-recording and re-peated reproduction of lectures need not necessarily be a bad thing if it releases staff time and energies for seminar and tutorial

19

language that the same two words should without further classification encompass and adequately describe the extremes represented by these two activities.

Simply to distinguish between the broadcast and the closed circuit varieties of television does little to clarify the situation. Nowadays, for example, medical programmes designed for the general practitioner are regularly broadcast both by the BBC and by many of the commercial companies. There is no appreciable difference in either style or intention between these programmes and the videotape recordings which are being used on closed circuit for undergraduates in some of our medical departments. Programmes broadcast to schools have in many instances over recent years come steadily closer to the concept of direct teaching, and we may even be approaching the danger of overlap – in intention, if not in content – between the work offered by the broadcasters and that presented by the larger closed circuit systems. One cannot yet say precisely what forms of teaching will emerge when the Open University becomes a reality; but it seems likely that they will draw upon conventional lecture-room techniques as well as on those of the broadcast studio. So the distinctions which it is important to make are not those which describe merely the method of distribution – highly relevant though that may be – but the more fundamental distinctions which derive from the aims underlying any particular educational activity practised by means of television.

The strictly logical approach might be to start from the simplest one-camera applications of television, and work outwards from that point to the instructional uses of television when it is operating as a means of mass communication. In practice, however, it makes sense to do exactly the opposite – that is, to start with the television that most of us know, and work from there towards the more specifically didactic context. Starting thus, of course, we start with broadcasting; and we look first at material which need not in any strict sense of the word be educational at all, for the main stream of broadcast television contains much that does not spring from any *intention*

The main studio in the Glasgow Schools system is just over a thousand square feet in area. With three cameras, telecine and videotape machines of broadcasting standard, it is designed for work of a professional level.

Children of most ages learn very quickly to ignore the cameras during sessions of classroom observation. Here they pursue group activities apparently undisturbed by camera or cameraman.

What was once a classroom in Queen Anne School, Dunfermline, has been converted into a remarkably efficient television studio. At the control panel is the school's television director (a teacher now wholly employed in this work); at the camera is the full-time television technician. Programmes can be relayed live to several classrooms simultaneously, or recorded for subsequent use.

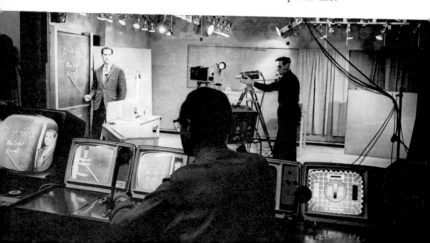

to educate. But programmes that are not educational in purpose can be educative in effect; and though both the BBC's Charter and the Television Act of 1964 speak of broadcasting as a means of 'disseminating information, education and entertainment', it is to our great advantage as a community that these three commodities should be regarded as elements which can often merge imperceptibly into each other rather than as mutually exclusive forms of communication.

It is this main stream of television – seldom educational but often incidentally educative – that provokes in the professional educator an attitude which is compounded of admiration, fear and envy. It provokes his admiration because of its sheer capacity to communicate, to establish trends and to build up personalities whether real or imaginary. His fear springs from the belief that much of our television promotes a wrong sense of values, and that much of the information it conveys is glib and superficial. And he is envious because here in front of the domestic receiver is the mass audience which, as he sees it, should rightly be available for education. His missionary spirit rises up in him, and he determines that here is an audience that should be reached and won – if only he can somehow fight his way into the broadcasting studios. Now any missionary faces challenges; and when the professional educator enters the field of television in search of his mass audience, the first challenges to be dealt with are those very characteristics of mass communication which inspired his admiration and his fear. He admired the sheer capacity to communicate: but now he must ask himself what creates this capacity. He will rapidly discover that it is neither the camera nor the microphone. To his probable discomfiture, he will also realize that it is something more subtle than simply knowing your subject. If he is brave enough and objective enough to submit himself and his colleagues to comparative experiment, he may well discover that the capacity to communicate to a mass audience by television has more to do with personality than with knowledge; and that the question 'Who shall communicate?' becomes just as important as 'What shall be communicated?'

So the very characteristic which he admired about broadcast television – its capacity to communicate – becomes one of his first problems.

You must remember, of course, that we are still following the fortunes of a missionary educator determined not only to use television but also to win the mass audience which he believes to go with it. The next challenge he faces is the characteristic that distresses him in much of what he views at home – the apparent superficiality of television exposition and discussion. This he fears and disapproves of: yet it is something he must come to terms with, if he is indeed determined to pursue sheer size of audience. He will learn that heated argument makes for more gripping television than does a cool and painstaking analysis. He will learn that a surprising amount of information will be accepted with interest if it relates to a controversy that is current tonight: though much of it will be forgotten or misinterpreted tomorrow, and will next week be resisted because the controversy is past and forgotten. What he is discovering, of course, is not something new; he is merely facing up to old facts seen in a new context. For the mass audience has much in common with the child – it is seldom captured by the logical approach, by the development of a subject from first principles and for its own sake; but it is always willing to be caught by the psychological approach, the seizing of a subject while interest is still warm, the unfolding of a story backwards from the news headline or the current dispute.

The missionary educator may at this point begin to have his doubts about the mass audience. He may even decide to settle for a more limited field where the pure principles of educational practice are less likely to be compromised. It would be a tragedy if he and all his colleagues retreated too readily from the challenge and the example of popular broadcasting, for there must be considerable (if not strictly measurable) social value in that broad sector of television output which is merely educative and not avowedly educational. 'Panorama' can teach as effectively in one sense as 'Parliamo Italiano' does in another; and the teaching impact of a documentary is not diminished by the fact that it owes more to the film cutting room than to the lecture theatre. One way or another our missionary will learn a good deal that he can adapt and apply within the conventional teaching pattern. He will no longer assume that any teacher can become a good television teacher, but will acknowledge that factors such as personality and flair enter into the choice of performers. He will still be unwilling to compromise with superficiality, but he will acknowledge that there are times when teaching – and not only television teaching – can legitimately draw upon journalistic and dramatic techniques.

But if his tentative exploration produces no other result, it will force him to consider more seriously whether it is really a mass audience that he wants to reach. The 'mass' audience is a passive animal, not ill-disposed but largely indifferent, prepared to show interest when titillated, but losing this interest rapidly when intellectual effort is called for. Its ambitions are strictly limited; and according to the mood of the moment, we are all a part of it. The mass audience, in short, lacks that very quality of involvement which is an indispensable element in the educational situation. It may be exposed to much that is *educative* – and may with benefit accept it – without ever being caught up in an activity which is *educational*.

Let him once discover and accept the characteristics of the mass audience, and the educator will probably agree that the target which television more realistically offers him is a 'very large' audience. This distinction, of course, almost certainly implies a difference in size; but the difference that really matters is one of quality and attitude. The audience for an educational television programme may, by normal teaching standards, be very large; but it is by definition an audience which is in some degree at least committed to the learning process.

Where then, in the broadcast field, can we draw the line of demarcation between educative and educational television? So far as adult programmes are concerned, a useful definition is offered in the formula which was agreed some years ago between the BBC and the Independent Television Authority. The 1962 White Paper on Broadcasting had expressed the wish that 'an early start should be made in providing more educational programmes for adults'; and the Government had offered additional broadcasting hours to allow for such programmes – provided that the BBC and the Authority between them could produce an agreed definition of their scope and intentions. And this definition was arrived at:

Educational programmes for adults are programmes (other than school broadcasts) arranged in series and planned in consultation with appropriate educational bodies to help viewers towards a progressive mastery or understanding of some skill or body of knowledge. The definition shall be held to include programmes primarily designed for class use (e.g. in technical colleges or in centres for adult education) and also programmes primarily designed for the home viewer.

Several points arise from this definition. The most fundamental, probably, is the insistence on a 'progressive mastery or understanding' of the subject being treated. The viewer is regarded as being no longer someone who is just watching a programme. He is now taken to be an individual who has committed himself to a course of study; and the fact that the programmes are arranged not as self-contained entities but in series implies sustained commitment not only by the broadcasting authority but also by the viewer himself.

However the arrangement of programmes in series has a significance that goes beyond the mere question of number and duration: it can affect the whole style and depth of the programmes themselves. Why has television gained its unenviable reputation for superficiality? Partly, as we have seen, because it is usually aimed at a mass audience and makes the concessions that are believed to be necessary on that account; but also because the individual 'one-off' programme normally attempts to be self-contained, to offer within its allotted thirty or forty minutes an account which has the appearance of being complete. The result, of course, is often that the treatment is complete only in programme terms – it has the semblance of being well rounded; it has a beginning, a middle, and an end; and the very expertise with which these are achieved can give the misleading impression that an issue has been well and truly dealt with. Allow that your educational programmes are arranged in series, that no single programme claims to do more than take a few steps forward, that there is time between each instalment for the viewer to do some work or at least some thinking on his own account, and you have moved substantially nearer a use of television which is actively educational.

But notice, too, that the formula agreed by the BBC and ITA stipulates consultation with appropriate educational bodies. There is no need to enumerate here the various committees and councils which advise our broadcasting authorities on this sector of their output; the significant thing is that such consultation is seen to be necessary and does take place. Write off some part of it, if you must, as merely formal recognition of various institutional interests: the fact remains that genuine educational television has to be seen as constituting only one part of a wider pattern, and it should be related wherever possible to the needs arising in the existing educational framework, and to the facilities offered by that framework.

So it follows logically enough that the agreed formula envisages some courses which will be designed primarily for class use, as well as those which will be geared to the home viewer. The distinction here is not merely nominal: a known difference in viewing circumstances – classroom as opposed to sitting-room – in turn affects the style of production, and a series designed to be accommodated within the curriculum of the technical colleges will have outlines more definite than one designed as the focal or inspirational point for a home viewer's own private study.

The categories and sub-divisions of educational television can already be seen to be multiplying. One thing they all have in common – that a vital part of the learning process lies outside the television programmes themselves: without in any way disparaging the effectiveness of the television element, one might almost say *the* vital part. It is a characteristic of all those series which have an expressly teaching purpose that they are supported by face-to-face teaching, or by discussion groups, or by relevant teaching notes and literature; and there can be little doubt that it is in the non-television parts of any course that real learning progress is made. Exactly the same applies in the more conventional composite learning situations: the university student who merely attended lectures would make little advance – it is in the personal study towards which his lectures serve as a guide that he pushes outwards the boundaries of his understanding. So it is not surprising that in recent years there has been a steady development of courses which take the idea of 'supporting literature' a step further – courses which are designed from the start as a fusion of television programmes with correspondence teaching.

So far, then, we have distinguished three types of specifically educational television for adults; and they correspond broadly with three degrees of commitment. First, there are programmes (with supporting literature) for those who wish to view at home and follow up with an amount of study which is entirely a matter of their own choice. By far the larger proportion of adult educational television falls within this category – one thinks, for example, of elementary language programmes like 'Komm Mit!' or 'Bonjour Françoise', both broadcast by the BBC; or of series like 'A Plain Man's Guide to his Money' or 'The Grammar of Cookery', which were carried by most of the independent companies. Their purpose, which is quite explicitly to teach, is tempered by elements of entertainment or sharpened by the very practical appeal of titles like the last two mentioned. Their target is the individual viewer, surrounded by the comforts and the distractions of his own home. Their effectiveness is not, in the nature of things, easily measurable; but their audience is known beyond all doubt to be a very wide one. Nor are such audiences merely passive. To cite only two striking examples: when a course in Russian was broadcast by the independent companies in 1966, the viewers who actually bought the supporting booklet numbered no less than twenty thousand; while one hundred thousand purchased the publication that accompanied 'The Grammar of Cookery'.

Second, there are programmes designed primarily for use in a class situation, or closely related to the type of work which might be covered in a course of day-release lectures. Within this category we have series like those designed by the BBC for use in technical colleges – courses in engineering, science and general studies. Similar in type, though different in context, were the thirty-seven programmes which Border Television broadcast as 'Farm '66' – a series which introduced to the uses of farm machinery young people who were just entering the agricultural industry, giving them in effect the equivalent of a day-release course (and, incidentally, the opportunity of qualifying for a City and Guilds Certificate at the end of it).

Third, there is the more limited number of series in which the viewer can simultaneously watch the television programmes and pursue a related correspondence course which is conducted by some body other than the broadcasting authorities. The first experiment of this kind was 'College of the Air' – courses in English and mathematics broadcast by Anglia Television and backed by correspondence from the National Extension College. Another early experiment was 'The Standard of Living' – a course in economics offered in the autumn of 1964 on the joint initiative of Nottingham University and Associated Television. A year later, the BBC in conjunction with NEC offered a course in statistics which was on broadly similar lines; and since that time there has been steady progress in this kind of co-operative effort. Although we are concerned here primarily with the use of television, one must note in passing that the development of radio-and-correspondence courses is equally vigorous; and there are certain areas of study – language, literature and music being notable among them – in which sound radio's freedom from the visual seems almost to be a strength rather than a restriction.

One further sub-division of adult educational television, as at present provided, remains to be mentioned: this is the increasing number of series directed towards clearly defined professional groups. Such programmes, though they are produced mainly on the assumption that they will be watched by viewers individually at home, take relatively little account of the accidental or fringe viewer who may watch by chance or out of general interest. They are primarily refresher or up-dating courses, prepared for a profession by members of that profession. Since 1963, for example, many of the independent companies have broadcast programmes for doctors in practice; and similar medical programmes are now also originated by the BBC. 'The Managers' was a BBC series dealing with industrial problems at managerial level; 'Dairy Farming Today' had as its target audience those who were actively involved in the care of dairy herds; and several series – like 'Children and Mathematics' or 'A New Approach to Biology' – have been designed to bring members of the teaching profession up to date with the newest methods being applied in their own subjects.

The degree of commitment implied by the expression 'educational television' is, therefore, a very variable quantity. At one end of the scale it may be the temporary and half-amused interest that the prospective holiday-maker shows in a French language course; at the other, it can be the professional involvement of the general practitioner in the latest techniques of the medical specialist. But few of our British television series, up to this point in time, have assumed or been designed for that level of commitment which leads on to any recognized qualification. This is not intrinsically a criticism of their value, since they are undoubtedly followed by many viewers who have an uncomplicated and disinterested desire to learn. Nevertheless one knows that motivation is strengthened considerably by the existence of a target; and this added element of motivation will be one of the distinguishing characteristics of the television

30

programmes which – before long, if promises are fulfilled – are to provide part of the teaching offered by the Open University.

The Open University (or University of the Air, as it has mis-leadingly been called for some years) will make use of television; but the proportion of the teaching actually given through television itself seems likely to be small. So far as one can see at the moment, the broadcast component of the new university's work should be closely comparable to those television-and-correspondence courses which have already been mentioned: but the new venture may provide us with a more objective assessment of television's teaching potential than has yet been available. Until now we have been able to measure the audience in terms of its size and its appreciation, and we have had the reassurance of the viewer's own conviction that he is gaining ground; but the effectiveness with which adults learn from broadcast television programmes – the effectiveness, that is, in any measurable form which could be compared with the exam-ination results of a college or university – this has been something that we could only guess at.

CHAPTER FOUR

Direct Teaching for Adults

In the previous chapter we referred to two emerging types of directly educational programmes for adults – those which assume the viewer's commitment to a related correspondence course, and those which are directed towards clearly defined professional groups. Although such courses are growing in range and popularity, and are followed by a significant number of viewing and listening groups as well as by individuals at home, comparatively few extensive studies of their effect are as yet available. The Open University – which must use largely similar methods – is soon to be with us; and with this development in mind it may be useful to look briefly at three of the earlier British experiments in the direct teaching of adults by television.

All three were essentially modest undertakings. Significant in the indications they offer; arduous in the amount of preparation they involved; important, each of them, as first steps in a new field; but modest in scale and in the number of students they provided for the analysis of results. Since the programmes were broadcast and freely available to the public, they undoubtedly reached non-captive audiences of considerable size: but their reactions we shall never know in any detail. In each case, however, we do have evidence based on the reactions of a group of committed viewers – people who were consciously submitting themselves to an educational process: and this evidence, though drawn from limited numbers, is sufficient to offer some guide lines for future development and some indication of the organizational and political problems which have to be faced if broadcast television is substantially to extend its role in the sphere of direct adult education.

Of the three experiments, the first two described are similar in that they offered teaching in specific subjects – economics and statistics – to any members of the public capable of deriving benefit from them: more particularly, to any members of the public who were also prepared to take the further step of pursuing the correspondence course which was simultaneously available. The third was offered (indeed is still being offered) explicitly to the medical profession: there is nothing to prevent the layman from watching, but the programmes are neither designed nor intended for him, and formal research on their impact has therefore been confined to the medical profession.

In the autumn of 1964, viewers in the Midlands were offered a television course in economics. This did not happen overnight. The preliminary stages were long and involved. But the essence of the matter was simple: the University of Nottingham's Department of Adult Education took the initiative in that they expressed their readiness to explore the potential of television in adult education, and the commercial television company covering that part of England (ATV) responded by offering to sponsor, produce and transmit a series of programmes. Agreement on the general proposal was reached in February of 1964. It was estimated that six months would be needed to prepare the course and all the ancillary material: and the programmes were scheduled to run from late September to late December.

But before turning to the mechanics of the course itself, there was the central question of the subject to be offered. Why was the choice economics? When Professor Harold Wiltshire (who was largely responsible for this experiment) answers that question, he is by implication stating some principles for

33

educational television generally [3]. Economics was chosen first because it is a socially important subject, important enough to justify the use of public money for a costly medium. Economics is a subject that can be broken down into fairly small sections, and therefore lends itself to some measure of programmed instruction. In addition, it is a subject inherently suitable for visual presentation because it is in large part a study of changing relationships – for example, one can well understand why a pair of scales was featured repeatedly as a sort of visual simile in the programme that dealt with inflation. Finally there was the practical consideration that economics has long been established as a subject in adult education, so that there was a substantial reservoir of teaching experience in the subject upon which to draw.

So the subject was chosen, and its title – 'The Standard of Living', but the course was not planned simply as a series of unsupported television programmes. Four interlocking elements were to be included: the television programmes; a specially prepared handbook; exercises to be completed by the students and marked by tutors; and personal contact – between students and tutor, and between groups of students.

There were thirteen programmes in all, each 20 minutes in length. Each programme was broadcast twice – on Sunday at midday, and again on Monday morning. In style the programmes were simple, straightforward pieces of direct teaching. The scripts were written by a team of four people – that is, four people working together on each script: two economists, an educationist who had specialized in problems of communication, and the professional television producer. They were conceived primarily as acts of teaching rather than as television programmes. They were not a series of distinguished lectures, and they were not – as their organizers put it – 'educational showbiz'. The actual presentation of the programmes was by one of the two economists who collaborated on the scripts – it was considered essential that the material should be introduced by someone involved in the subject, someone who could feel the material to be his own, and not simply acted by a professional presenter.

What was the particular function of the television programme as distinct from the other elements in the course? It was to introduce to the student each week one part of the subject, to arrest and engage his attention by establishing and exploring connections between his own everyday experience and the particular economic principles which were being examined. Each programme also, of course, made a first journey through the material for that week's study and offered some analysis of it, but its primary purpose could be described as the building of a bridge between the student's practical experience on the one hand and economic theory on the other. This linking of theory and practice was reinforced, in most of the programmes, by introducing a visiting expert – the economic adviser to a bank, the managing director of a large chemical manufacturing firm, and so on. In style, then, the programmes were of the simplest. A presenter (professional in his subject, but not as a television presenter); a guest speaker, expert in a branch of economics appropriate to the programme; graphs, captions, animated captions, newspaper headlines – but an absolute minimum of the television trimmings associated with a programme for the non-captive audience.

It is impossible to say how many people may have watched the programmes simply as casual viewers, though a reasonable estimate puts the figure somewhere between 30,000 and 50,000; and one does not know what teaching if any was conveyed to this chance audience. The course was designed for people who were willing to add some active study to the relatively passive business of watching the television receiver. Such students were invited to enrol, at a fee of 10s. for the course, and those who did so received a handbook specially written to complement the television programmes. More precisely, it was written to cover the material of the first ten programmes, because preparation of the last three was wisely held over until students' work in the earlier part of the course indicated what approach was most relevant in the final stages. Each chapter in the handbook covered the same topics as one of the television programmes. The same ground was covered, and all the important diagrams used in the television version were reproduced in the book; but it was possible to include also more statistical material than could readily be shown on the screen. The handbook's purpose, briefly, was to take the material originally seen on the screen, underline it, consolidate it, and build around it. Just how much was built around would depend on the student, for – in addition to re-presenting the television material in written style – the handbook offered a list of recommended textbooks, and the students were sent the page references relevant to each week's study.

The economists who prepared the television scripts also prepared the handbook; programmes and written text were therefore expressly designed for each other. And the same team devised the third element – the exercises, which for convenience were printed as part of the handbook. At the end of each chapter was a tear-out sheet on which were printed the exercises for the week. In most cases there were about twenty objective questions (of the true/false or multiple-choice type), and there were two or three open-ended questions that demanded brief statements in reply. Programmes, it will be recalled, could be seen on Sunday or Monday morning. Study of the relevant chapter presumably followed. Exercises had to be in the post by Tuesday evening; and they were returned with marking and comments about nine days later.

Those who organized the course – and few educationists would disagree with them – regarded the exercises as the real pivot of the series. For one thing, the positive effort of completing the exercise made fruitful the relationship between the first impact of the television programme and the more intensive study demanded by the printed text. For another, the exercises involved the making of decisions – itself an educative process in any field.

So there were programmes, handbook, and exercises; but

there was a fourth element – the tutor. 'The Standard of Living' was broadcast by ATV in the Midlands; and economists on the staff of universities and colleges in that area were engaged as tutors for the students who enrolled in this course. Without going into excessive detail, one can say that in the event each tutor had about 43 students to deal with. The tutors' role was, first, to mark and comment upon the replies to the open-ended questions in each exercise. Implicit in their function was the idea that by their comments they should give further instruction, should encourage students to keep on working, and help them over difficulties when they arose. In addition to this purely correspondence contact, students were offered at least two occasions on which to meet their tutors – once after six programmes had been transmitted, and again after the tenth programme. These meetings, where the tutor met his students as a group (they were grouped geographically of course), lasted about two hours: they served two purposes – the tutors reviewed points which the exercises had shown to be causing difficulty, and the students raised questions on which they wanted to have a fuller exposition. That these meetings also gave an opportunity to students of meeting each other was considered by the organisers to be a further advantage, though one may question whether meetings so few in number can really have had any marked influence on the effectiveness of the course.

It has been convenient to speak as though all the students of this economics course were individual students working on their own at home. The great majority of them were, and the comments and conclusions offered later will refer to these individual students. However one must complete the picture by saying that over three hundred students enrolled and worked as members of groups in schools and colleges – working, presumably, under some degree of compulsion and supervision. In addition, another thirty groups of the same kind followed the television programmes and used the handbook, but without taking part in the correspondence element of the course.

So much for the nature and organization of 'The Standard of

Living', one of the earlier British experiments in the direct teaching of adults by television. Its costs, its results, and some of its lessons will be considered later in this chapter along with those arising from another experiment along the same lines – 'Mathematics in Action'.

'Mathematics in Action' [4] was in several respects similar to 'The Standard of Living': each course was a planned fusion of television teaching and correspondence. But here the joint sponsors were the National Extension College and the BBC; and, although similarities existed, there was one very substantial difference. Whereas 'The Standard of Living' was from its beginnings envisaged as a unitary television-and-correspondence course, 'Mathematics in Action' was designed in the first place as a series of schools broadcasts which would in any case have had its place in the schedule of BBC schools programmes. It was a series planned to cover a number of topics on the application of mathematics outside the regular school-examination syllabus: that part of the course with which we are concerned dealt with statistics. In level, the series was aimed at the final year of the secondary school; and the broadcasts were appropriate to young people who had just recently taken 'O' level mathematics.

Discussions between the NEC and the BBC led to agreement that the College should plan and provide correspondence courses linked with this series: and in April 1965 the planning of both the programmes and the correspondence element began. The programmes – ten of them, each of 20 minutes – were broadcast from mid-September to early December. There was very full co-operation between the BBC and NEC. Television scripts and indeed the pre-recorded programmes themselves were seen in advance by those preparing the correspondence course. But the statistician whom the NEC commissioned to write the course did so in relation to an already existing set of programmes which were not created as an integral part of the whole. It was natural, then, that the form of the course should be largely dictated by the nature of the BBC series, which was experi-

38

In the university, much television work will continue to be 'incidental'—a relay from the laboratory or pre-recorded case material will be seen within the framework of the conventional teaching pattern. This lecture theatre is equipped for television illustration as occasion demands.

This scene demonstrates the complementary roles of television lesson and class teacher. Blackboard work and television presentation are related and integrated.

If teaching by television is to be effective, technical standards must be as high as those to which children are accustomed in their home viewing. This glimpse of Glasgow Schools studio through the control room shows six technical and production staff—and others are involved elsewhere on telecine and videotape.

mental in its approach to the teaching of statistics. The intention was to get away from the traditional introduction to the subject, and to plunge straight into questions of sampling and probability. The subjects covered were – statistical inference; probability; the binomial distribution; hypothesis testing; sampling variables; normal distribution; experimental design; correlation.

Wherever it was possible, the correspondence course used the same illustrations as were used in the television programmes; and the printed lessons, of course, followed week by week the same topics as the broadcast series. With each correspondence lesson was a worksheet, to be returned to a tutor on completion; and students were given a further reading list with detailed references appropriate to each week's programme. Like every BBC schools course, 'Mathematics in Action' had an accompanying handbook available for purchase; this partially overlapped, naturally, with the correspondence course but was written at a different level.

Since the nature of the BBC series was predetermined, and since the programmes themselves were recorded in advance, it was an obvious difficulty that students' reactions could not sufficiently be taken into account as the series progressed. To overcome this difficulty at least partially, two extra programmes were added for the correspondence students – tutorial programmes as they were called. These were placed one at the middle and one at the end of the series; they dealt with problems that were seen to be common to many students, and one of the tutors for the correspondence course took part in each of them. (This arrangement offers an interesting parallel with the tutorial meetings which formed part of 'The Standard of Living'.)

In style, these programmes too were direct acts of teaching, as practised by the BBC in such a context. A single presenter carried all the programmes (with the tutor appearing in the two tutorial editions), and the material was extensively illustrated. The exercises in the correspondence course, it would be fair to say, were more active affairs than those for 'The Standard of

39

Living' in that they involved to a greater extent the working of problems, and depended far less on the objective question to check assimilation. The correspondence course, in fact, was written at a level described as being 'distinctly more difficult than the related television lessons'. In other words, students were being asked to watch the television exposition of the subject at one level, but to carry out their private study and their exercises at another and higher level – a technique which may have wide implications.

It has seemed worthwhile to describe the organization of these two television-and-correspondence courses in some detail, since they may well prove to have set a pattern which will come to be widely adopted. 'Teaching through Television' [3] gives the complete background to the economics course, while the statistics course is fully covered in 'Correspondence Teaching and Television' [4]. And now, a look at the results of both series – starting with 'The Standard of Living'.

One is anxious not to complicate this account by quoting excessive statistical detail, but a few hard figures should be given to indicate the basis on which any comments are founded. The programme, one must recollect, was available to the Midlands only. 3,065 people bought copies of the handbook – indicating at least their intention to follow the course, if not to take part in it fully. 1,656 of these people also enrolled for the correspondence course: of these, some 300 were working as members of groups in schools and colleges – leaving the 1,347 individual students who form the real basis of our comment. Of these, 867 completed questionnaires after the course was over; and their answers provided additional background information.

How well did the students stay the course? Of the 1,347 who enrolled, 228 apparently went no further. But of the remainder, 49 per cent did all the exercises set; 68 per cent did ten or more; and 77 per cent did eight or more. We describe adult education students as 'effective' if they attend at least two-thirds of the class meetings and complete the written work required of them.

Taking this definition as a measure, we can describe 77 per cent of the economics students as effective – whereas in the same area of the country at about the same time, only 74 per cent of ordinary adult education students were in the same sense effective. Over half of the students bought or borrowed books for further study related to the course. Most spent from one to two hours a week in reading, and completing the exercise. About two-thirds of the students attended the first meeting with their tutor; one-third attended the second (but it had unwisely been arranged to take place just a day or two before Christmas).

Fifty-five per cent of the students were men, 45 per cent women – whereas adult education classes in general attract more women than men. Does this mean that economics has a greater appeal for the male, or does he simply prefer to take his education in private? The age distribution, on the other hand, was closely similar to that found in adult education classes generally: the television group in fact was slightly younger than one would normally find at classes, but there was a bunching of students in their 30's and 40's which is typical.

We must remember that we are dealing here with one relatively small group: but, with that reservation, an interesting fact emerges about the educational background of the students in this television course. Those with minimum educational qualifications appear to have been attracted to it in greater numbers than they are attracted to the conventional adult class. 38 per cent of the students had left school between the ages of 13 and 15; 25 per cent had left at 16; and although many of them had previously attended classes in practical and recreational subjects, liberal adult education was something new for most of them. Only one-sixth had ever attended anything in the nature of a university extra-mural class.

What about cost? Disregarding altogether any fringe viewers who may have watched the programmes, one can consider the complete course as having been provided for 1,650 students (including those who worked in groups). The entire cost, including printing and the notional remuneration of those who

D

compiled the course, was £24,700. The surprising thing about this is that when one calculates the cost of running conventional adult classes for the same number of students – scattered, let us suppose, over the same geographical area and meeting in groups of about fifteen – the total cost comes to about £21,450. Add that the fee for enrolment and the handbook was by any standard incredibly low; consider what the effect might be if a similar course were run on a much larger scale – and patronized proportionately, of course; and one begins to wonder whether the cost-per-student of such a television-and-correspondence course need be regarded as extravagant. (At the same time one must recollect that this course was run within a region, not nationally: the fact that it was regional may have contributed to its local appeal, and one must not too easily assume that extending the distribution area would so multiply the number of participants as to bring a sharp decrease in cost-per-student.)

Turning now to 'Mathematics in Action', the BBC–NEC course: the actual number of students from whom conclusions can be drawn is smaller than in the Nottingham experiment. 277 students enrolled, about one-third of these as members of groups (that is, studying under a teacher), and two-thirds as individuals. But comment is based on only 134 students on whom full background information was available. This is indeed a small number from which to draw any firm conclusions: so let us speak merely of indications.

Men students outnumbered women by something like four to one. Again one is struck by how untypical this would be in the conventional adult class. Here, too, a bunching of numbers in the 30's and 40's – with 41 per cent in the 30's, 30 per cent in the 40's. (Perhaps it is straining a point to draw attention to the fact that here, as with economics, the balance is on the younger side?) There were quite clear groupings among these statistics students so far as the nature of their full-time jobs was concerned. The three largest groups were – schoolteachers, people engaged in work study, and accountants. The factor general to these and to many other students was that they now felt the

42

study of statistics to be increasingly important in their jobs, though they had not studied it when first qualifying for their professions. About half of the group had at least one university degree, or were qualified teachers, or held membership of a professional association. However there was also a proportion of students for whom formal education had ceased at an early age – 10 per cent had left school at 15 or earlier, and many had had no full-time education since the age of 18.

As with the economics course, so in statistics there was no final examination: no marks can be quoted as a measure of success or failure (and even if they could, would they mean much in relation to a group starting from so many levels of previous knowledge?). So we look once more to the completion rate as some measure of the course's achievement. How did they stay the course? Using again our definition of the 'effective' student as one who attends at least two-thirds of the meetings and completes the written work, 50 per cent of the statistics students were effective. The small group who left school at 15, with no subsequent full-time education, did better than those who left school at ages 16 to 18. But the dominant factor in completion of the course seems undoubtedly to have been motivation. Of those who were already finding the need for statistics in their jobs, 80 per cent were effective, of those who felt that they 'might one day use statistics', only 60 per cent could be so described. The age of the student seemed in this experiment to be irrelevant to the degree of persistence with which he followed out the course.

There was a wide variety in the amount of time which students reported themselves as devoting to work on the course – from less than an hour to over seven hours weekly. The average (for what it is worth) was $2\frac{1}{2}$ hours spent on the weekly lesson, and a further $1\frac{1}{2}$ hours on background reading.

And what was the cost? We cannot directly compare the cost of the economics and statistics courses because of their quite different organization. In the case of this BBC–NEC experiment, the BBC programmes were being produced in any case

43

and paid for out of the schools broadcasting budget. The correspondence course was a separate and financially self-contained affair. Individual students paid £4 each for the course; students working in groups paid less. In the event, the total expenditure on 277 students was £1,100 – but it must be stressed again that this was the cost of the correspondence element only.

Now that the facts and figures about these broadly similar courses in economics and statistics have been set out, it would be reasonable to go ahead and draw some inferences – which indeed we shall do. But before coming to that point, let us look at a third and quite different course of television teaching; after which we can suggest some of the indications and the question marks that arise from all three.

The two courses already described were undertaken as experiments. 'Post-Graduate Medicine', which started on an experimental basis in 1963, has long since passed that phase and is now an established feature. It is, as its title implies, a series of programmes designed for general practitioners; and it is one more example of collaboration between an educational institution and a television company – in this case, the Post-Graduate Medical Board of the University of Glasgow on the one hand, and on the other Scottish Television. The target audience has been neither the public in general nor any mixed group of committed viewers: the programmes are aimed wholly at the medical profession. Other universities are now co-operating with Glasgow in the production of these programmes; and, although transmissions were originally seen in Scotland only, recorded repeats are now carried by commercial companies in most parts of Britain outside the London area. However research has until recently been pursued in Scotland only; consequently in this survey it will be simplest to speak as though this were a purely Scottish project seen in Scotland. Any comments, in other words, are derived purely from Scottish practitioners.

'Post-Graduate Medicine' was designed to meet the situation

in which only a small proportion of doctors attend any form of refresher course after graduation. The problem is partly that of arranging courses suitable in time and place and partly that of securing a changed attitude to further education within the professional field. So when Scottish Television offered facilities for producing and transmitting programmes for the general practitioner, the opportunity was welcomed as one way of reducing the practising doctor's isolation, encouraging his interest in further study, and bringing him up to date with recent developments. Each programme is devoted to a single topic – for example backache, thyrotoxic conditions, glaucoma. The style has been absolutely straightforward – normally two or more clinical teachers take part, dealing with complementary aspects of the topic, or representing conflicting views on treatment. Occasionally a general practitioner also contributes, as a questioner or offering illustrative material from his own experience in practice. Patients are interviewed, or examined, as appropriate. Styles of presentation have included straight-to-camera exposition, carefully prepared interviews, and discussion groups. Extensive use has been made of captions, diagrams and stills, and there has been a limited but steadily increasing use of film. Planning and scripting has been entirely a medical responsibility; and though to the lay viewer they have sometimes lacked polish, and perhaps been something less than 'good television', they must be judged as what they set out to be – medical men speaking their own language to medical colleagues.

At the time of writing, an extensive survey of the effectiveness of these programmes has been undertaken; but this research work is only now in progress. Available at the moment are the results of very limited research carried out in some areas of Scotland only; and any comments made here are, as already pointed out, based on groups of Scottish doctors – one group of 432, and another of 781 [5]. From these groups, however, there emerge some reactions of value to us not so much as comment on this series of programmes in particular, but as indications of the attitudes of professional people to educational television programmes which are prepared specifically for their own profession.

To begin with, a few pointers to the value that doctors place on this opportunity to have some sort of refresher course in their own homes. For some of their programmes, scripts were made available to doctors on payment of a small fee. 55 per cent of the doctors answering a questionnaire said they would be glad to pay for illustrated scripts – many were prepared to pay for scripts even without illustration. Two points here – willingness to pay, which signifies a degree of commitment: and, once again, an appreciation of the printed word as reinforcement of the television programme.

Questions on quite a different topic produced similarly favourable answers. Doubts had at times been expressed about broadcasting on an open channel programmes designed for the medical profession: and, when asked about the hypothetical use of scramblers which would give them private reception of their programmes, 67 per cent of the sample group of doctors said they would be willing to pay up to £10 for a scrambler service – some were prepared to pay even more. The significance of these answers, however, allowing for the context in which the question was asked, is not so much that doctors were demanding privacy for their programmes, but rather that they were expressing their appreciation of the broadcasts – that they were prepared to *pay* for them.

Some doctors have, however, expressed misgivings about the effects on the layman of watching the programmes – the usual fear being that patients might become hypochondriacs and a nuisance to their doctors. This fear (admittedly confined to a small minority of doctors) is apparently ill-founded. In practice, the programmes contain a good deal of medical and scientific jargon, as they should, and this is having the effect one might expect upon the lay audience – commercial television audience measurement for the series originally estimated a total audience in central Scotland of some 200,000, but three years later the figure had dropped to a mere 20,000.

Some interesting indications arise from examination of the age groupings in this entirely professional body of viewers. Here, as in the quite different courses described above, there is a marked bunching in the 30's and 40's – but very markedly in the 40's. In this context, too, perhaps, it is in the late 30's and the 40's that a man becomes conscious of the need for retraining, for a re-charging of the batteries. Two other age-linked trends are worth noting. First, that it was in the higher age groups that disapproval of the programmes *in principle* was most often expressed: a fact which can be variously interpreted, but one encouraging and not unreasonable deduction would be that younger doctors (in their 20's and 30's) are favourably disposed to the idea of further professional education, prepared to accept it by television, and not averse to sharing it with those lay-men interested enough to have the programme switched on. But if younger doctors do not disapprove in principle of the programmes, it is their age group which is most critical of the programmes' production and presentation. Over 40 per cent of the doctors in the group under 30 were dissatisfied with these aspects of the series – the presentation being criticized more than the production. In other words, they were complaining not about the actual teaching content of the programmes but about the style in which the teaching was put across. An age group that has grown up with television, one might argue, is unwilling to accept anything less than 'television standards' of performance even in a strictly teaching context.

Research so far conducted and reported has suggested some trends only, confirmed a few reasonable hypotheses; but it has been confined almost exclusively to matters of quantity and opinion. Two much more difficult questions remain to be answered – how much knowledge do doctors acquire and retain from such programmes; and what ultimate effect, if any, is there on the viewers' daily practice of medicine? In short, we have reasonable evidence in medicine as elsewhere, that television programmes are watched, welcomed, and are believed to fulfil a valuable purpose: evidence sufficient to justify our continuing with them. We have not yet devised any dependable way of isolating and measuring their real effect.

It would indeed be rash to pontificate on the basis of these three courses. Though they were all adventurous in their conception, they were – by broadcast standards – modest in their scope and in the size of their audience. However their results do offer some interesting indications, and prompt a few questions.

The two television-and-correspondence courses did not *prove* that some element other than the television programme is necessary as part of the teaching process. Both were courses designed on that reasonable assumption – but it remains an assumption. Only research conducted on two comparable courses, one with and one without correspondence, could establish that the correspondence element was indispensable. Nevertheless it remains a reasonable assumption, to which most of us would subscribe, that the television part of such a course equates broadly with the lecture content in a university course – it can, depending on the subject, provide the inspirational element; it provides periodically a focal point for one's study; it offers at least one version of personal contact with a teacher. But in the end it is the regular exercise of the material studied that makes it a student's own. This is no new discovery, nor is it any criticism of television as a teaching medium: it is merely a healthy reminder that television has not fundamentally altered the process and the principles of learning.

Another common-sense reminder that emerges from both the economics and the statistics courses is that every available opening should be left for adaptation of the television material – or the correspondence element, or both – as an educational course progresses. Where television is the nearest one gets to teacher–student contact, it seems foolish to render any available feed-back ineffective simply because an entire course has been pre-recorded. Every possible space must be left for the introduction of material in response to the obvious needs of the students – in both television and correspondence elements if possible.

Professor Wiltshire, who organized the Nottingham experiment, wrote subsequently: 'Not much will be achieved if we merely try to attach a correspondence course or a series of class meetings to a pre-existing television course which somebody else has planned.' As the organizer of an admittedly successful course, he must be regarded as more entitled than most people to his opinion: and yet there is surely room for doubt? We are all accustomed to basing a teaching course on the pre-existing textbook which has been planned and written by someone else: need we regard the television course so very differently? And on financial grounds alone, one cannot help feeling that in a country where there already exist television services offering schools programmes up to near-university level, there is a very substantial justification for a pattern such as that employed in the BBC–NEC experiment in statistics. Taking that argument one step further, consider the significance of the fact that the NEC course offered correspondence instruction at a level rather higher than that of the television course. If the television programme can effectively be used as the focal point for a course running at a different level, could it equally be used as the focal point for courses running at several different levels? If so, one could envisage basic television courses being used to service a variety of correspondence courses, not merely of different levels, but slanted appropriately for a variety of professional requirements. Keeping to statistics as our example, a television course could serve as a core for correspondence courses that meet the different specialist requirements of the teacher, the accountant, the small businessman.

It has already been pointed out that there is a frustrating lack of any qualitative assessment in the results of these television courses so far. Students completed this or that number of exercises, but how good were they when they had finished? We do not know, but we do know how much they say they studied. In the economics course, most students spent one to two hours a week reading and writing their exercise, but to those of us accustomed to university work this seems a ludicrously low figure. Is there a danger in adult television teaching (a danger common perhaps to various forms of adult education) that students will *think* they have studied a subject when in fact they have been picking at the merest fringes? Here again we have a criticism not so much of television teaching as of any system which does not lead to a final qualification of some recognized standard.

On the question of cost, two points should be made. There is a tendency, since the arrival of television, to speak too exclusively of television. We should be looking much more closely at the possibilities of allying television and sound radio. Once granted that you are introducing the correspondence course as an element in the situation – with the extensive possibilities of illustration that it offers – it may be that some parts of a course can be carried with economy and even with positive educational advantage, on radio rather than on television. The second point is this: that self-marking techniques (which are wholly acceptable in the case of any serious student) could, if they were more extensively used, effect an economy in tutors' fees and could also substantially reduce the gap between performance of an exercise and the correction of one's errors. (Nine days, as in the Nottingham experiment, is a long time to leave errors uncorrected in the student's mind.)

Both the economics and the statistics courses gave the indication – really nothing more – that television courses may appeal to slightly younger age groups than do conventional adult classes. Does this signify anything? Possibly that as educationists we should be considering especially the broadcasting of educational material for those in their late teens and 20's – an age group who (for the time being at any rate) look on television as something 'of their own age'. Having said that, one must recall that it was the young doctors who were most critical of indifferent production and presentation. Which may well suggest that, for this younger age group in general, programmes must be good television as well as being good teaching.

But what constitutes 'good television' in this context? Perhaps more than anything else the unselfconscious use of the medium: for this younger age group, after all, television is not something new – it simply *is:* they are irritated by constant coy references to the wonder of the medium, to the terrors of appearing on it: and like their elders they are also irritated by irrelevant attempts in a serious programme to ape those television techniques which are only appropriate to the quite different uses of television as a medium for light entertainment.

This leads naturally to another point on the style and technique of the direct teaching programme. The evidence, both from the experiments under consideration and other sources, and from commonsense as well, is that an audience which really wants to study, to work, wants to do just that; it is not interested in visual frills and trimmings. In the case of the statistics course, for example, shots of pigs and squirrels were used at various points to illustrate sampling techniques: but such illustrations were written off by many students as a waste of time. This reaction is worth noting, because we who are engaged in television may easily be carried away by an almost obsessional degree of illustration. Over-illustration, the introduction of material because it is 'televisual', can be an affront to the serious student and a positive distraction from the teaching aim of the programme. Nevertheless within its own boundaries any act of teaching committed to television must be fully professional *as a performance* if it is to be effective.

As educationists we are always clamouring for our fair share of broadcasting time and facilities; but are we always quite sure what we are asking for, and why we are demanding it? The educationist who breaks into the field of television may do so as a merchant; or (as we saw in an earlier chapter) he may do it as a missionary. As a merchant, if that is his choice, he will be offering courses that some people – a relatively limited number of people – feel a need for. Thus a fairly small number of

51

viewers will recognize the value of a course in economics, because they want to understand the economic side of political argument, or because they believe it will help them to make the best use of their money. Similarly, small groups – mainly of professional people – will value the provision of a course in statistics and will be prepared to buy it from the educational merchant who offers such a course on television.

One likely characteristic of such groups is that in any one locality they will be very small, though they will be geographically widespread and perhaps quite evenly spread. For example, professional people who now need re-training or additional training (like the teachers who felt the need for statistics) will be scattered, one here, two there, forming altogether a sizable group but one ill-suited to the conventional idea of gathering in adult classes. So when the educationist turns to television as a means of teaching such a group, he is certainly not seeking to use it as a mass medium. Is he, then, looking to television because its techniques and its facilities will improve his teaching? Apparently not: one characteristic common to the three experiments we have looked at was the straightforward style of presentation, the relative freedom from frills and gimmicks, and there is even the suggestion that students resented such minor frills as there were. The fact of the matter seems to be that where the teaching of more or less specialist groups is concerned, the educationist – in his capacity as 'merchant' – is looking not for a mass medium, and not for a reservoir of new techniques, but purely and simply for a distribution system.

That a broadcast channel ideally offers such a distribution system is beyond question: that the educational merchant should seek his outlets where he can get them is what we must expect. Whether it is an acceptable arrangement that broadcast channels, created for wider purposes of public entertainment and enlightenment, should at times become simply a distribution system for the teaching of specialist groups is another question altogether. One is not condemning the use of television as a distribution system, far from it: one is suggesting that this function should be seen as a separate one, probably deserving separate facilities. One is adding a reminder to the educationist that he should ask himself in any one set of circumstances *why* he wants television – as a mass medium? – as television, with the facilities peculiar to television? – or simply as a convenient distribution system?

However, the educationist may approach television in the missionary spirit. The truth of the matter is that in recent years he has approached it in a rather confused state of mind. He has seen it as a mass medium, he has been aware of the vast audiences that follow sport and drama and light entertainment, and has sometimes assumed that – given the same cameras and the same receivers – he could achieve the same audience for education. And his sorry fate is that, advancing upon television as a missionary, he finds himself overnight a merchant with very few customers for his wares. The distinction, of course, is an old one: it is merely sharpened by the arrival of a new medium. Given the necessary degree of motivation an audience will accept the most direct forms of teaching – from books, from a lecture, from unadorned television. If a man *wants* to learn – and this is true whether he is a small farmer learning to keep his books, or a teacher catching up on statistics, or a doctor keeping abreast of the latest techniques – he neither needs nor wants to be cosseted along with every adventitious trick that television offers.

The educationsist can, like the originators of the three series we have been examining, decide to use television as a channel for absolutely direct teaching. On this television front he is challenged not so much by his audience (which is willing, committed, or captive) as by problems of distribution, and of keeping under control a medium whose facilities can be almost too profuse for strictly educational purposes. The paradox is that television as a mass medium offers the educationist a second front where he meets completely different challenges and must to a large extent use different weapons. He must be clear at any one time which front he is facing; too often we are not.

CHAPTER FIVE

Broadcasting to Schools

If we turn now from adult programmes to schools broadcasting, and particularly to the television element in that broadcasting, we have a rather different set of circumstances. The adult programmes we have been considering are planned in collaboration with various educational bodies, and sometimes geared quite closely to the known requirements of, say, the technical colleges. But the general understanding on which adult programmes are produced is that the great majority of the audience will be viewing individually, in a non-captive situation. Though viewing groups exist – and this may well be something that will develop considerably with the advent of the Open University – and though television courses have frequently been used as the central theme for the regular meetings of an adult class, it remains true that relatively few adults are likely to follow a series within any framework more formal or more compelling than that of their own personal interest.

The schools producer, however, works in the knowledge that his audience lies within an existing and well-established educational framework. Because he is working on broadcast wavelengths, he is always likely to have a large eavesdropping audience including many adults; but his primary target is one of schoolchildren working within this known framework, and working towards quite clearly defined levels of scholastic attainment. What is more, these children can be expected to be viewing in class groups and under supervision. In that sense the schools producer has a substantially captive audience, and might be considered to have an easy and well-ordered assignment.

To leave the matter there, however, would be grossly to over-simplify the picture – if it is a picture of schools television in Britain that we are trying to assemble – for the provision of schools broadcasting in this country can best be described as a 'typically British' arrangement. The British-ness of the system can best be recognized by looking aside for a moment – and not necessarily with greater approval – at the quite different French organization. In France, all schools television program-mes are prepared by the National Pedagogical Institute – a body which was set up by the Ministry of Education for research and for the production of teaching materials. Within this Pedagogical Institute, television programmes are prepared by a specialized team which is attached to Radiodiffusion-Télé-vision Française. Now RTF itself is, of course, a government service responsible through the Ministry of Information to the Prime Minister's office. So you have two government services working together on programmes for an educational system whose control is already highly centralized – even to the extent that through the whole of France every grade (in all but the private or religious schools) is taught the same subject at the same hour on the same day. Collaboration between the Pedagog-ical Institute and RTF takes place at all stages of planning and production; but in effect schools television programmes are seen through from start to finish by educators who are all a part of the government service.

Here in Britain there is greater diversity in both broad-casting and educational organization. There are as many schemes of work as there are local education authorities, and as many time-tables as there are schools – a fact which militates against the widest use of schools programmes, and must therefore imply the frequent waste of expensive television resources. On the broadcasting side, too, there is a diversity of programme originators. So far as radio programmes for schools are concerned, the BBC remains the sole provider – as it has been since the late 1920's – but when the BBC was ready to offer television programmes to schools, the Independent Television Authority and its companies had already arrived; so there has never been a monopoly of television schools broadcasting. Since 1957, in steadily increasing quantity, programmes have been prepared for the schools by both the BBC and the various independent companies; and the situation is still further diversified by the fact that within the BBC some separate schools series are offered in Scotland, Wales and Northern Ireland.

Diversity can, of course, be a highly commendable feature in any form of organization; and in this country we cherish particularly the local freedoms of our educational system, at least so far as the actual content of the teaching is concerned. Nevertheless one is bound to wonder whether, in the matter of both the production and the use of schools television, we have not accepted too complacently a diversity which is in practice unjustifiable on economic grounds. The elements of the situation, simply, are these: schools television programmes are produced by the BBC nationally, and in separate series for the three national regions; they are also produced by half a dozen of the independent companies; but all these programmes are transmitted in the uncertain hope that they may by chance or by local goodwill fit into the infinite variations of the individual school time-table.

One consequence is that in the secondary schools both radio and television are used considerably less than in the primary schools – it is in the secondary school that the time-table becomes most complicated and inelastic; and yet it is in these same secondary schools that the shortage of fully-trained specialist teachers might best be alleviated by the use of television. Technically, the dilemma might be resolved by the videorecording of programmes for use at a time to suit the school's own time-table; this is now common practice in the case of sound broadcasts. Legally, there are still objections to one's doing this with television programmes, though it is to be hoped that these may shortly be overcome, but financially one must be realistic: how many schools can afford the equipment – very broadly speaking, it would cost about £1,000 – to videorecord schools programmes off transmission?

In short, we have not really and effectively come to grips with the common sense and the economics of schools television. It is a field in which our insistence on educational freedom may well be leading us into an extravagant half-use of expensive technical resources and scarce specialist talent. However this must not be allowed to develop into a treatise on the organization of schools broadcasting. It is more to our immediate purpose to examine the style and intention of the programmes offered; and here the picture is a good deal simpler, though steadily changing. We have already seen that educational television can mean a variety of things in the adult broadcasting sector: is it an equally various term within the field of schools broadcasting?

The answer is, probably, that it is not so much a question of various types but of varying emphases. Long before the arrival of television and the subsequent creation of the Independent Television Authority and its companies, the BBC had established so solid a background and so wide an experience of schools broadcasting in sound that any television development in this country was bound to bear some family resemblance to that original model. Now since the earliest days of sound programmes for schools it had been emphasized that there was no question of the broadcasts supplanting the teacher. In 1935, with schools broadcasting already well established, we find the newly appointed Secretary of the Central Council for Schools Broadcasting insisting that 'the broadcast talk does not brush the teacher aside: it offers what the best teachers are constantly seeking, a link between the school and life outside, between the classroom and the home' [6].

This idea of widening the horizons, of breaking down the school walls, has largely persisted throughout four decades of schools broadcasting; almost as persistent is the theme that the broadcast never replaces the classroom teacher. A year after the 1957 start of the BBC's experimental Television Service for Schools, we find this official comment: 'The aim of these programmes, as in sound broadcasting, is to supplement the work of the teacher by using all the resources of television, such as specially shot film, studio presentations, dramatic productions, and outside broadcasts, including the use of the Eurovision link' [7]. Three years later, in the BBC Handbook for 1962, there is still the same insistence – 'As with sound radio, the aim of school television is not to provide lessons, but to supplement established methods of classroom teaching by exploring the educational possibilities of the medium' [8].

In view of this repeated stress on the merely *supplementary* nature of the television programme, and on the necessity for its depending essentially on the resources peculiar to the medium, it was natural enough that the schools television programme should come to be regarded primarily if not wholly as a matter of 'enrichment'. There was a time when the broadcasters were willing enough to have their programmes so described, when they had no misgivings about insisting that their programmes must escape from the atmosphere of the classroom. So in 1960, still in the early days of schools television, a Unesco commentator could justifiably write: 'British children compare school television to entertainment television rather than to school lessons. Producers therefore seek to avoid any resemblance between school television and the school' [9]. A few months earlier, the BBC's School Broadcasting Council had said of current affairs programmes that 'it is the descriptive film which the children enjoy most and recall most readily; discussion of the issues themselves is much less exciting visually and much more demanding intellectually' [10].

Programmes of the enrichment type are still with us, and indeed they form a substantial part of the total schools television pattern; but the description is no longer considered so acceptable as it once was – use it to a group of schools broadcasters nowadays and the atmosphere will become wary if not openly defensive. Some will suggest that 'off-syllabus' is a less misleading label, one which admits that the programme may not be contributing directly towards any qualifying course yet does not imply the suggestion of mere educational frills. Nevertheless, the word is likely to survive its current unpopularity: it will remain a useful shorthand description for that broad category of programmes which – by dramatic reconstructions, by the extensive use of film and outside broadcasts, and not least by the employment of skilled professional broadcasters – can give television teaching an impact and an authority which remain beyond the reach of the individual teacher. For financial reasons alone, if for no others, the enrichment programme which fully deploys the resources of television is likely to remain the province of the broadcasting networks; it will lie well outside the budget of any local authority's closed circuit system.

No one would deny the value of the enrichment programme in itself, though there have always been teachers who are prepared to wonder whether an undisguised appeal to the pupil's enjoyment really has all the teaching value that is claimed for it. Look back at the 1959 School Broadcasting Council's report which is quoted above – 'It is the descriptive film which the children enjoy most . . . discussion of the issues themselves is much less exciting visually': was this to be taken as suggesting that enjoyment and the peculiarly visual capacities of the medium should be exploited at the expense of the real teaching purpose, which was presumably the 'discussion of the issues themselves'? Surely not: yet there did seem in the early years to be some danger that in 'exploring the educational possibilities of the medium' producers might not always hold the balance evenly between the 'good television' that would satisfy the purists among their broadcasting colleagues and the good teaching which was the strictly practical requirement at the classroom end.

In the last few years there has been a clearly discernible shift in emphasis, a shift away from the purely enrichment idea and towards more direct teaching. Several factors have contributed to this change. For one thing, there is nowadays less strength in the conviction that television can never replace the teacher. True, it may never be regarded as desirable to replace the teacher; one may hope that broadcasting will continue to supplement his work in the classroom rather than supplant it. However, experience in countries less fortunate than our own has shown how extensively television can, in fact, take over in the field of day-to-day classroom teaching.

In Italy, for example, since 1961 television teaching has been used to provide regular courses of lower secondary-level instruction for children living in small communities with no secondary school. Signora Puglisi, the Director of Telescuola (whose achievement in the teaching of adult illiterates has been much more widely publicized) explains that for this secondary school work she had 'to consider the television medium far more in the light of a means of long-distance communication than from the point of view of its possibilities as spectacle, for these – though very valuable in auxiliary education for regular schools – were distracting and ineffective in our case' [11]. The pupils who receive their daily lessons by television meet at viewing centres under the supervision of teaching assistants, and have their homework corrected by correspondence. No one claims that this is by any means an ideal situation, but the fact is that to a large extent it works. In circumstances where there is an acute shortage of specialist teachers, these pupils are – through television – still taught by specialist teachers; and 80 per cent of them pass the same State examinations as their contemporaries who have the benefit of more orthodox face-to-face teaching.

It may still be the ideal that broadcasts should never replace the teacher; just as important, it may still be politically unwise to suggest that they can even partially replace him. Yet here in Britain the element of direct teaching by both radio and television is increasing and becoming more explicit. Recall the earlier quotations from BBC policy statements, and compare them with this from the 1965 BBC Handbook:

Some school broadcasts offer an enrichment of the normal curriculum by providing an imaginative experience which may serve as a useful starting point for further activity. Others, especially in music, have for some time attempted more direct instructions, because of the shortage of trained subject teachers. Recently, teachers have particularly welcomed a directly instructional contribution from broadcasting in the field of science.

Though this comment referred in particular to radio programmes, the change in emphasis applies equally to television, where there is an increasing provision of direct teaching programmes in those fields where we are experiencing a shortage of specialist teachers, or where new teaching methods are emerging. Notable among these at the moment are the fields of mathematics and physics, where television programmes are serving the dual purpose of directly teaching the pupil and simultaneously offering a form of 'in-service' training for the teacher who is relatively unqualified, or unacquainted with the latest methods of presentation.

How far is it possible to categorize school television programmes? The exercise is to some extent an artificial one, and one to which the broadcasters do not explicitly commit themselves; but we can reasonably distinguish a few general types, and impose certain theoretical classifications. These demonstrate, if they do nothing more, the broadly ranging alternatives that lie between enrichment and direct teaching and which frequently, of course, include some elements of both.

The provision of personal experience: this is the characteristic and the role of many schools television programmes. The experience may be aesthetic – a glance at the week's programmes, current at the time of writing, shows 'The Art of Music' with passages from Bach and Elgar concertos; while 'Drama for Sixth Forms' offers excerpts from a Pinero comedy.

Or the experience provided may be more practical, in the sense that a film or an outside broadcast takes the pupil on a real-life visit to people and places outside the range of his own daily contacts. This same week's programmes, for example, take the sixth form to the National Engineering Laboratory, while younger groups inspect the assembly line of a large car factory or visit the United States. To such direct experience, whether aesthetic or practical, a commentator or anchor-man may add whatever element of didactic material seems appropriate.

These direct-experience programmes supply the context, the true and real-life context, to what might otherwise be a purely classroom study. But a second type of programme attempts to achieve similar effects by building up an imaginary context and supplying a reconstructed and imaginary background – a task which radio achieves more easily and more cheaply, no doubt, but which is nevertheless frequently undertaken by television. Turning again to this week's schedule for an example, one finds a history programme sub-titled 'Freeman and Serf' which 'introduces some of the people who lived and worked on Sir Robert Faldrey's manor'.

What one might call 'active response' programmes form a third identifiable group. Here the broadcast calls for activity on the pupil's part: it may be some simple physical activity such as we associate with the long-established 'Music and Movement' programmes on sound radio, or it may be the con-junction of physical and mental activity involved in imitating or carrying through to its conclusion a science experiment suggested by the television programme itself. The classroom teacher here remains vital to the teaching situation both in preparation and in follow-up; but her function may be almost completely taken over by the television programme while it lasts.

Then there is the 'stimulus' type of programme which is designed, with the long-term co-operation of the teacher, to start off a chain reaction of activity in project fashion. Though normally aimed at the pupil, essentially the same type of programme may be prepared with the teacher in mind. 'Improvised Drama', for example, a series planned for secondary school teachers of English, examined ways of encouraging teenagers to develop an idea and spontaneously translate it into active dramatic form.

Earlier generations can recall those welcome if infrequent occasions on which the school assembled to hear at first hand the experiences and the views of some visiting notability. The contemporary equivalent is a broadcasting commonplace, whether on sound or on television; and the 'visiting expert' type of programme, if we can call it that, offers a particularly vivid way of providing the context and the background to classroom study. Still taking the same week's schedule as our random sample, we find among the billings a research physicist and a distinguished actor – either of whom would have merited star treatment had he visited a school in the old days.

Next there are those series – call them 'oblique approach' if you must have a label – which break down or at least ignore the normal school subject barriers: easiest to describe generically as current affairs or modern studies, they include elements of history and geography, politics and economics; and they have the considerable educational strength of building a bridge between the classroom and the child's outside experience of home viewing, of newspaper reading, and (if he is fortunate) of informed adult conversation.

But nowadays, as we have already suggested, there are also series which set out quite openly to provide the basis of subjects which are a normal part of the curriculum. Though they depend on the co-operation of a classroom teacher, they are in themselves unquestionably direct teaching, and they cover all stages up to sixth form work. It is manifestly inadequate, then, to suggest simply that there are two types of broadcast television for schools – the enrichment and the direct teaching varieties. Though these terms are useful as indicating two extremes of intention, they fail to classify with anything like sufficient accuracy all the varieties of purpose that lie between

63

them. This is yet another instance in which the rapid growth of television has outstripped the capacity of our vocabulary to match it. But putting the niceties of vocabulary on one side, the significant development in recent years has been the steady progress of the broadcasters towards direct teaching. Significant, because it implicitly accepts that the practical requirements of the educational situation are at least as important as theories about the nature of the television medium; because it raises, increasingly, questions about the relative functions of the television teacher and his colleague in the classroom; and because it is in this very area of direct teaching that overlapping and conflicts of interest could most easily develop between the broadcasters and the larger closed circuit systems like those in Glasgow and London. It is to these much more recent arrivals on the television scene that we turn our attention next.

CHAPTER SIX

Area Closed Circuit Systems

Something like half a dozen local education authorities in Britain are now operating, developing or investigating closed circuit systems to cover the schools under their control. One hesitates to be more precise than that, because it is an area of such rapidly growing interest that a few months can mean the addition of several more names to the list. Hull and Plymouth were early in the field; Edinburgh has plans for its own network within a year or two; and the Inner London Education Authority is committed to a very substantial scheme, part of which will begin to operate in the autumn of 1968, while the system will gradually build up to its planned completion in 1970.

However, the first full-time local authority system to work on a regular daily schedule was that in Glasgow. Opening on the 30th of August, 1965, it has had pioneer experience of both the problems and the possibilities inherent in such an undertaking; and, though in a few years' time it should be overshadowed in size by the ILEA network, Glasgow meantime provides the obvious model for the description of what one means in practice by local authority closed circuit television. First, some physical details. At the centre of the system – and, incidentally, very near the centre of the city – is one very adequate studio, with space already earmarked for another. The one studio at present in use is just over a thousand square feet in area, has three cameras, facilities for transmitting film and slides, and two videotape machines of full broadcasting standard. It is – and this is an important point – a studio professionally designed for work which is, in the technical sense, of a professional level. This should be clearly understood: the closed circuit systems of which we are speaking – that is, local authority systems covering a large area – differ from broadcasting in their method of distribution, but they are not to be regarded as television's 'poor relations'.

From Glasgow's central studio, a cable network of about a hundred miles in length spreads out to all parts of the city: more precisely, it stretches out to reach 315 schools and Further Education Colleges. Operating to begin with on one channel, the system now uses two; and another two can be brought into service later on if this proves to be necessary. In the schools are 27″ receivers which offer both BBC and ITV broadcasts as well as the locally originated programmes – initially two receivers in each of the city's senior secondary schools and one in each of the others, though it seems obvious that the number of monitors provided in the schools must increase if the system is to achieve anything like its full potential. It would indeed be a strange economy to arrange for the possible reception of four different simultaneous programmes, and then to eliminate that possibility by providing only one receiver.

If we are realistically to assess the educational value of such a project, we must see it in its whole context; and one element in the context which we cannot dodge is the question of financial outlay. So how much did all this cost? Reconstruction of the building which was to become the central studio – it was already owned by the authority – consumed some £65,000; and if work goes ahead on a second studio in the same building, about half that amount would cover the additional construction. Both the studio equipment and the entire distribution system are held on a rental basis. Rental charges, staff salaries, fees to television teachers, and every incidental recurrent expense down to cleaning materials – all these added up in the first full year to slightly less than £80,000. The estimate for the second year, allowing for some expansion of the technical facilities, rose to about £108,000. If these figures seem daunting to anyone unaccustomed to the financial commitments of a large city, they must be put into perspective. Glasgow has a teacher force of around 7,000; and its annual bill for education is, broadly, £31,000,000.

By comparison with the amounts of money involved and the size of the potential audience, the staffing of an educational television centre seems small. Glasgow managed to get off the ground with a permanent staff, administrative and technical, of only ten. The explanation, of course, is that the burden of the teaching work and its preparation is carried by teachers seconded full-time or part-time. Whether such an arrangement will continue to work satisfactorily in the local systems, or whether the purely television teacher is likely to emerge, is a question to which we shall be returning.

The Inner London system will vary from Glasgow's in some technical details – the precise type of cable distribution, for example, will be different and it will allow for six channels; but in most other respects the two should be closely comparable. Except, of course, that London's educational television centre will be transmitting to a much larger number of schools and colleges – almost 2,000 schools and over 50 colleges of various kinds. The potential schools audience alone will be in the region of 400,000.

So much for the hardware, the cost and the sheer numbers, which are impressive enough; but how does one use such a system? In Glasgow, the main concentration initially was on modern mathematics and spoken French. The mathematics programmes – algebra, geometry and arithmetic – were undertaken because specialist teachers in this field were facing the current demand for new elements in the course and the emergence of new teaching techniques. The target audience was the first year of the secondary school, so it was possible for the programme to start right in at the beginning of a new syllabus. Aimed at a purely local audience, the programmes were scripted and presented by Glasgow teachers – practising teachers, not specialist television 'performers'. Three of these mathematics programmes were presented each week, constituting together about a quarter of the total time allocated to the subject in the individual school's time-table. The wide variety of time-tables in a city as large as Glasgow presented a problem, of course, and this was met as far as possible by transmitting each programme at five different times in the course of the week.

In style, the presentation is quite straightforward direct teaching, addressed through the camera to the pupil in school, there is no question of teaching a class in the studio. Pupil participation is encouraged and indeed assumed; it is built into the mathematics lessons by the inclusion of questions (with pauses during which an answer can be given to the classroom teacher) and the posing of problems which the pupil is asked to deal with by writing in his jotter.

The spoken French programmes, which were the other main constituent in Glasgow's original pattern, have been aimed at the primary school, thus breaking almost entirely new ground so far as Scotland is concerned. Half of the output here has been taken up by the transmission of the Heath de Rochemont film series 'Parlons Français', and the other half by programmes produced in Glasgow and aiming at the same age level as the films. The locally produced content rests mainly on the presentation of songs and little plays; for these, pupils from various schools in the city are brought into the studio to take part, and these dramatic activities offer the framework and provide the context for relatively informal teaching of the spoken word. Direct teaching? – well, it's a matter of definition. At all events, the mathematics and the French lessons represent two quite different ways of using the television system, each geared to its own particular purpose. As with mathematics, so the French programmes have been transmitted repeatedly – each episode is scheduled four times in the week.

68

In addition to these two main series, the Glasgow service even in its earliest months offered a variety of single programmes on subjects ranging from science to social studies and from road safety to the Fire Service. Explicitly for teachers, there was a course of lecture-demonstrations in the Cuisenaire method of teaching number. At twenty-minute duration, each of these talks was transmitted first during the lunch break and again at the end of the school day.

The general intention, subject to the lessons of experience, is that the teaching offered by this television service should gradually extend upwards and outwards – upwards, in that mathematics teaching originally given for the first year of the secondary level will steadily work its way up the school syllabus; outwards, in that the range of subjects will be increased as demand and suitability dictate. Further possibilities of extension in scope are offered, both for the later stages of secondary work and for the in-service training of teachers, by the fact that two-way cable links exist between the central studio of the schools system and the studios at Jordanhill College of Education and the University of Glasgow.

Now it is easy to be either carried away by enthusiasm – or, alternatively, thoroughly alarmed – when one is introduced to the extent and the potential of the big-city closed circuit system. Caught up in either reaction, we may not stop to ask just why such schemes have been embarked upon. Even when seen in their proper perspective, the financial outlays are still very substantial: on what grounds did they seem reasonable at the time of their inception, and is experience likely to show that they were justified on those grounds or on others? By 1963, when the first real stirrings of interest began in Glasgow, school television broadcasts had already been proving themselves for almost six years – proving themselves effective in many ways, but also showing the disadvantage of network planning which could not be closely geared to local requirements. This partial dissatisfaction, however, could scarcely in itself be the reason for such major expenditure – we had, after all, been managing without television at all for a very long time. Nevertheless school broadcasts *had* planted the idea of using television, and had at the same time shown that broadcasting alone (at least as it is presently organized in this country) could not begin to supply all the subject choices and variations of approach which television theoretically made possible.

So the television idea was there; and 'because it's there' has often seemed a good enough reason for the exploration of some new opportunity. There was undoubtedly an element of adventurous experiment among the educationists who launched the Glasgow scheme; but experimental approaches in the educational field have seldom been encouraged by the expenditure of local authority money at the rate of some £80,000 annually: surely there must have been some more hard-headed considerations involved? There were. Glasgow, as we have seen, has a teaching force of around 7,000: at the time in question it also had a teacher shortage of around 1,300. The salaries that would have been paid to the missing 1,300, had they been available, would have come to a total far in excess of the annual expenditure on a television service. This juxtaposition of an unwished-for economy on the one hand and a relatively small but adventurous outlay on the other is something that cannot have escaped the City Fathers.

Add to the shortage of teachers in general a particular scarcity of specialist teachers in the mathematics and science field, and you had a situation in which something had to be done. It was not unreasonable to suppose that television in the course of time might make a substantial contribution towards solving this problem, which seemed likely to be a persistent one. None of this is to be taken as suggesting that closed circuit television was introduced directly as a way of circumventing the teacher shortage – on all hands we still hear the view, first propounded by the broadcasters, that the classroom teacher can never be replaced. However, somewhere there must have been the beginnings of a conviction that gross shortage of teachers and the unexplored

70

Television makes it possible to conduct psychiatric interviews in the privacy of a small consulting room and relay them to a class of students elsewhere in the hospital. They may also, as here, be recorded for future study.

An example of ingenuity in the original small closed circuit installation at Notre Dame College of Education. An ordinary 16-mm. projector is used for film inserts, the projected image being picked up by the Lynx camera in the foreground. The success of this do-it-yourself studio has led to the planning of a more elaborate and conventional system for the college.

Portable videotape machines like this have proved their value in universities and colleges of education. The monitor here shows close-up detail of a chemistry experiment which has been recorded on the machine.

potential of television were two factors in the whole educational situation which might usefully be brought to bear upon each other.

With that, surely, as a perfectly legitimate background consideration, what are the expressed objectives with which a local authority system comes into being? Two main purposes emerge, and this is how William Beaton, first director of Glasgow's Educational Television Service, expresses them: 'One was to complement the basic day-to-day work of the schools through direct-teaching programmes deliberately geared in content and pacing to school curricula; the other was to provide a continuing in-service training of teachers in the rapidly changing content and methods of many curricular subjects' [12]. With that as a cautious and general statement of the main aims, let us look in greater detail at the probable benefits of local schools television.

For a start, it is obvious that the local output can be very closely related to the syllabus which applies in that area; this has never been possible with the national broadcasters. We may not all approve of the extent to which variations exist between one local education authority and another; but they are there, and network broadcasting cannot possibly take account of them. Not every authority wants to introduce spoken French in the primary school: Glasgow did, and only the existence of its television system made this effectively possible. Not every authority decided simultaneously to introduce the new mathematics, nor is every teacher adequately equipped to teach the subject: again, Glasgow's system made possible both the system and its implementation. It is perhaps at the upper end of the secondary school that this direct relationship between local television, local syllabus and local requirement will become most valuable. With a steady increase in the sub-division of subjects, and a related growth in the number of subject choices available, closed circuit television may prove to be one realistic way of dealing with small numbers of specialist pupils scattered in a large number of schools.

Our thumbnail sketch of Glasgow's ETV makes a second advantage immediately obvious – that a local system (particularly if it is a multi-channel system) makes it possible to repeat programmes much more frequently than can ever be the case with BBC or ITV; it is probable, too, that transmissions can be placed in accordance with known time-table trends throughout the city. This flexibility is well demonstrated by some figures from Glasgow's first year of operation. Throughout the session 220 programmes were produced, but the number of repeat showings was such that actual transmissions reached a total of 1,479. In the nature of things, the broadcasters – working on single channels and meeting many other commitments – cannot begin to compete with figures like these, which will rapidly multiply as time goes on.

Local syllabus and local demand for specific subjects have already been mentioned, but local relevance, too, can be an important factor in teaching; and this should prove to be a particular strength of the city television systems. This applies in all the casual local allusions which add impact and intelligibility to daily teaching – Sauchiehall Street and the Broomielaw mean nothing to the London child, though they are vivid points of reference to his Glasgow contemporary; and it applies with equal strength in the matter of organized local studies. Teaching that is related to the conditions and problems of one's own neighbourhood is, on balance, likely to be more effective teaching; this is true of a lesson in the classroom, and it is reasonable to suppose that the same principle will apply to the various forms of television lesson that may develop.

Next there is the question of feedback, of audience research, of ascertaining that the output is appropriately geared to requirements and is in fact satisfying the needs of the target audience. The broadcasters rightly pay a great deal of attention to this aspect of schools work, and the BBC's education officers are continually engaged in the objective assessment of school broadcasts and the reporting of classroom reactions to them. How well organized and how effective is feedback likely to be in the local systems? This, if we are not careful, could easily become one of the 'ha'porth o' tar' economies of local authority television. Granted that speedy and informal reactions are much easier to collect throughout a city than on a national basis; granted that meetings of local teachers can be arranged (and the enthusiasts will attend); granted that personal comments are more likely to be conveyed to a local performer; it still remains surprising that after two years' operation there is no formal machinery for assessing the effectiveness of Glasgow's television teaching. In the matter of speedy feedback – speedy enough to make a difference to next week's lessons – all the natural advantages would appear to be on the side of the local service: but findings that are to be valid and objective must, for a start, be organized. On that score, for the time being at any rate, the points must go to the broadcasters.

Some particular benefits are likely to result from the use of city television circuits in relation to the various types of college involved. Both Glasgow and Inner London include the further education colleges and colleges of education in their systems: London's transmissions will also reach schools of art, technical colleges and colleges of commerce. Wherever day-release work is involved – as in the further education colleges – it is common practice for teachers to repeat identical lessons and demonstrations on several days each week. Only those who have been caught up in this soul-destroying process can fully appreciate the deterioration that marks each successive performance; and it is to be expected that many such teachers will welcome the opportunity that television offers of recording those parts of their teaching which would be just as effective when played out centrally from videotape. The inter-availability of a television system between schools and colleges of education has several advantages, the most obvious among them being the ease with which teachers in training will now be able to study and analyse one form, at least, of teaching in action.

Much of our emphasis so far, too much perhaps, has been on the organizational advantages of a city system: yet these may never be very far removed from the strictly educational benefits. And high among these benefits is the chance that local television offers of using visual resources far more varied than are ever likely to be available to the ordinary teacher, yet without going to the sort of financial outlay that could only be envisaged by the national networks. The use of specially shot film, the imaginative manipulation of photographic stills, the inclusion of animated captions and of skilled graphic work generally, all become economically possible when programmes are being prepared for a complete local authority area rather than for a single school. Not only do they become economically possible, but the television service will inevitably include in its staff the specialist artists and cameramen whose skill it is to present in visual terms the points that a teacher, all too often, has been trained to formulate only in words.

The individual teacher, whether in school or in college, tends to become academically inward-looking; he has little opportunity in practice to compare his techniques and ideas of presentation with those of his colleagues. One of the incidental advantages of the local television situation is that it is bound to bring teaching methods under more continuous and more conscious scrutiny than has ever been the case before. This works in two ways. First there is the simple fact that the teaching given by one small group (those appearing on television) is laid open to observation and criticism by a city-wide audience of their colleagues. It does not follow at all that the television lesson will be accepted as an ideal example of teaching method; but in practice the mere possibility of observing and criticizing someone else's approach to a subject is virtually certain to stimulate fresh thought about one's own. So there is a real probability that the local television service will (quite apart from programmes specifically prepared for teachers) revitalize teaching in the area: not necessarily or even chiefly by the imitation of television methods, but simply because a new awareness is created that there *are* different ways of presenting any given body of material.

If this is to be a benefit gained by the profession in general, it is one experienced in a very marked degree by those who are actually involved in preparing the television lessons. To take Glasgow again as an example of what will probably become fairly general practice, programmes are prepared not by one individual but by a panel of specialist teachers in the selected subject: and it is discovered in practice that the sheer process of preparation, with exchange and mutual criticism of ideas, is itself educative. What matters, of course, is that it should lead to better teaching: and early evidence suggests that it does. Some of us would argue that one major benefit of the preparation-and-production process is lost if the final direction in the studio is also carried out by a specialist teacher in the subject concerned. The objective eye and ear of an 'outsider' can at this stage make a contribution which should not lightly be discarded: but that is something to which we can return when we examine the related roles of teacher and producer.

Finally, in this round-up of the benefits likely to result from local schools television, we must add one more which is a wide-open question mark. It seems perfectly possible that television will present us with new teaching techniques we haven't even thought of yet: but we will only discover them if we use it. At the moment our use of the television mechanics still hovers uncomfortably somewhere between the entertainment medium we have grown up with and the classroom methods that were established long before we came on the scene. As we become less self-conscious about our new acquisition, we are more likely to see the ways in which it can best change, or be changed by, established teaching practice.

The arrival of the local education authority systems raises a few broader questions of policy – some of them interesting primarily to the television professional, others to the teaching profession; while some indeed should be matters of very general concern. Take a television point first. The commissioning of these local systems represents a recognition of television first and foremost as a *means of distribution*. Many ancillary benefits will follow from its use, and we have indicated some of them, but the repeated emphasis on direct-teaching methods, albeit with television's added visual resources, implies that the chief attraction of a city system has been its capacity to make available to many schools the teaching that would otherwise have been restricted to a few. This acceptance of television's purely distributive function is almost certainly a healthy development; it will at any rate diminish the mystique that has inevitably grown up around television as an entertainment medium; and it will counterbalance the enthusiasm of those purists who argue that nothing should be done on television unless its expression is so necessarily visual that it could not be done in any other way.

By all means let us recognize the role that closed circuit television can play simply as a system of distribution; it may well be that we should give more active consideration to the use of broadcast wavelengths in the same way. But if we are to employ television at this utilitarian level, we must make quite certain that a change in use is not confused with a change in standards. In this country, though we do not always fully appreciate the fact, we are accustomed to the very highest technical quality in broadcasting: subject only to the vagaries of their home receivers, our pupils have been conditioned to accepting nothing less than top quality pictures. It is therefore of considerable importance, in the educational television system, to eliminate the possibility of unfavourable comparisons and to get the technical aspects of production absolutely right. This is no field for the amateur. One may argue the case for and against the fully professional performer in the local service, or for the teacher-director as opposed to the television professional: but on the engineering side there can be no argument. A teaching programme that is marred by frame rolls, indifferent picture quality, intermittent or distorted sound, is one that might as well never have been produced. Direct teaching that is being cabled around the city must be as polished technically as enrichment teaching that is broadcast across the country.

Next, an issue that mainly affects the teaching profession – the exact nature of the teacher's involvement in the whole complex of a local television service. There has in the early stages been a general insistence that this new use of television must be seen as an activity in which he is conscious of personal participation, a system which he can himself help to mould. 'An ETV service for teachers by teachers' was adopted as the slogan in Glasgow; and, well in advance of Inner London's opening date, E. W. H. Briault, ILEA's Deputy Education Officer, was echoing the same sentiment – 'It is regarded as of the utmost importance that the Authority's closed circuit television service should be developed in response to needs identified by the teachers themselves and in close co-operation with them' [13]. Dr Briault went on to speak of teaching programmes 'worked out in consultation with the receiving teachers and presented by teachers seconded for this purpose full or part-time for limited periods'. Now such sentiments are entirely laudable, but they imply involvement of two quite different kinds – consultation on the one hand, active participation on the other. Consultation can obviously take place at the city level in a quite vital and productive way: that the teachers of any given subject are al speaking about the same syllabus makes their comments more immediately relevant than they would be in similar exchanges at a national level. So the individual teacher, if the machinery for consultation exists and works satsfactorily, may well be conscious of influencing the trends and emphases of the television teaching.

This in turn should favourably affect his attitude to classroom participation, to preparing his class for the television lesson and to following up the instruction that he has had some share in planning. But when all is said and done, the element of consultation and participation in which the average teacher is likely to be involved must remain peripheral. Active participation – that is, in membership of the subject panel that prepares a programme, or in the actual television presentation itself – is bound to be restricted to relatively few. Membership of the advisory

77

panels is something that can over the years be shared by a good many teachers: but what about television performance and direction? Is this something which, for the sake of a slogan, should be shared around and around? – or are we prepared to accept the emergence within the teaching profession of a new type, the full-time television teacher?

This is no idle question, set up merely for the purpose of academic argument. It will become a practical issue. There would be general agreement that the lessons should be taught by teachers – and by teachers working within their own subjects, not merely mouthing a prepared script. However, not all teachers are good teachers: asked individually to recall the really effective teachers in our own personal experience, most of us could accommodate them comfortably on the fingers of one hand. And not all good teachers are capable of becoming television teachers – they may turn out to be a new breed. Broadcasting experience suggests this. Why do we see the same faces so regularly on our screens at home? Sometimes because producers are lazy; sometimes because the faces have been placed under contract; but mostly because the man who can take a television camera into his confidence, without embarrassment to himself or his viewers, is the exception rather than the rule.

One probability must certainly be accepted by the teaching profession, however unpalatable it may be: that the most highly qualified man, or the best classroom teacher, may not prove to be the most appropriate choice for television presentation. Academic qualifications and long classroom experience should contribute to the planning of a series and the preparation of a script; but within the studio they may both count for less than that television flair which is so difficult to define but so unmistakable when we see it. One way or another, 'regulars' will find their place in closed circuit work just as they do in broadcasting; and it will become a matter of policy whether they continue to work on part-time secondment or are allowed to develop as full-time professionals in the new art of television teaching. It will be time enough then, perhaps, to worry about the particular status and salary scale which should be awarded to the teacher whose special skills are made available to a class that is numbered not in tens but in thousands. However it is settled, the administrators will have to evolve a formula which ensures the highest quality of studio lessons without sacrificing goodwill and general acceptance of the system by the profession in general.

What sort of style should the local systems develop in their television presentation? A ludicrously general question, since the style of any individual programme will depend on the subject and the age group: to take two cases that we have already quoted, spoken French for primary schools will naturally adopt an approach quite different from that of new mathematics for secondary schools. And yet one can give some general answers. 'Educational television,' says E. W. H. Briault, 'ought not to be classroom teaching televised' [14]. He is probably right; although in Italy one has seen effective television teaching where children have been brought into the studio just so that it *will* be a classroom atmosphere that is broadcast. The conditions in which Telescuola operates are rather different; and in this country the style should probably combine the simplicity, informality and directness of classroom teaching with just that amount of additional visual resource material which is immediately relevant – and no more. Television must not be allowed to run away with itself; the strictly defined teaching purpose must remain the dominant factor. In general, so far as style is concerned, local television should accept and even make a feature of its difference from the broadcast entertainment variety; but when we reach the stage of having local programmes for all age levels in the school, we shall probably find it best for the difference to be almost imperceptible at the infant stage, becoming more and more marked as we work our way upwards through the age and ability groups. The analogy of the printed word is not inappropriate: the infant's reader can with advantage bear a strong resemblance to the picture book he has left at home, but an intelligent adolescent will resent a textbook

79

that has been tricked out to look like a strip cartoon. So, in television teaching, the transition from pre-school viewing like 'Play School' and 'Watch with Mother' should be gradual, but definite.

Since the broadcasters are nowadays moving closer to the concept of direct teaching, there may be areas of broadcast and closed circuit work which come to resemble one another closely: which raises the whole question of the relationship between the broadcast networks and the local authority systems. How should this develop?

It must be our concern as rate-payers, licence-holders and educators, to see that their roles are complementary rather than competitive. The peculiar advantages of the local system, which are implicit in much that has been said already, themselves mark out the areas in which such a system should chiefly operate. The city television service can best handle those subjects, or those stages in a subject, whose teaching is closely affected by the nature of the locally adopted syllabus. It can cope with partic-ular specialist shortages. It can meet purely local problems, such as an influx of immigrant children, just as it can develop its own line in local studies.

What the local service cannot hope to undertake is the really wide-ranging project involving extensive travel (for which it has neither money nor staff), the dramatic production with pro-fessional actors, or a documentary based on expensive library film. On the grounds of expense and of professional expertise alike, these must be left to the broadcasters. It would be easy, in fact, to hasten to the conclusion that enrichment is the appropriate field for broadcasting, while direct teaching should be left to the local systems. And this might be a very satis-factory solution – but only for those few large cities which are within sight of making such a division of labour practicable. In the meantime the broadcasters rightly feel it their responsi-bility, for the sake of the majority, to advance into some of those fields (new mathematics is a case in point) which the local system has already shown itself to be perfectly capable of tackling.

There is one area in which fruitful co-operation between the national and the local systems is at present frustrated by legal and contractual considerations. A valuable broadcast programme, transmitted once or twice, may for time-tabling reasons miss a large part of its target audience. An 'off-air' recording made at the educational studio could make such a programme available on closed circuit at times known to be suitable for the local audience; but to make such a recording from a broadcast transmission – or, more accurately, to reproduce it for other than very strictly limited purposes – can under present conditions be an infringement of copyright and performance rights. The re-transmission of a specifically educational programme would, of course, merely further the teaching intention of the original broadcast; and it is to be hoped that a way may soon be found around the considerable complications which for the time being prohibit it.

If we were to pursue this question of the respective roles of broadcast network and closed circuit system, and follow it to a purely theoretical conclusion, one might envisage the gradual outward extension of local authority services to the point where a two-tier system had established itself – the national broadcast networks supplying what they are most appropriately equipped to provide, the local systems meantime expanding to offer perhaps regional coverage of direct-teaching requirements. There is indeed reason to suppose that within a few years' time the pattern of local government will become increasingly regional, in which case such an expansion of the authority systems might be regarded as administratively tidy; but strictly in terms of technical feasibility and educational desirability, is such a development really likely?

So far as desirability is concerned, the arguments are pretty evenly balanced. Any local television system, as we have seen, represents a substantial outlay and sizable annual expenditure; if such a financial load (and the studio facilities which it acquired) can be shared with neighbouring authorities, then expansion would make good sense economically. If it is an argument in favour of the local system that it extends the availability of the highly skilled teacher, then – in theory at least – any increase in its effective area should be welcomed as extending that availability even further. Against that line of argument, however, one has to weigh those very factors which appear to operate most strongly in favour of the tightly-knit local system. If local syllabus, local relevance, local studies, local acceptability are the things that matter, these are all advantages which would diminish progressively as the system grew larger.

What does seem reasonable and possible is that certain series – presumably those without any marked local relevance – could be exchanged on tape between one authority's system and another. Given that syllabus variations could be adjusted, the fundamentals of chemistry – and even of English literature – must be largely similar whether they are being taught in London, in Hull, or in Glasgow. But notice that we have named three large cities: not simply because they are three of the places that are already committed to closed circuit television, but because they *are* large cities. Local systems may well multiply in those authority areas which coincide with the conurbations; but it is very much less likely that they will spread to, or be established in the county areas which lie around them. The reasons for this are technical and economic. In large cities the school density is high; no one school is very far from its nearest neighbour; so the cable links from school to school are relatively short, and the rental or capital cost of the whole cable system is proportionately low. Glasgow's network stretches about a hundred miles, but it covers 315 schools and colleges. Translate a hundred miles of cable into the county or rural situation, where one school may easily be five miles from the next, and how far will it get you?

The unhappy fact is that the big-city television systems, desirable as they are in themselves, seem destined to create a still wider gap between the educational 'haves' and 'have nots'. The big cities have their teacher shortage and their scarcity of specialists: in their case, closed circuit television is both practicable and economically feasible, and in addition to meeting the immediate administrative problems it will bring peculiar educational advantages of its own. The rural areas have their administrative problems too: they are not immune from the shortage of specialist teachers and, if one is to take wider social considerations into account, it can well be argued that their need for television teaching – on administrative, social and educational grounds alike – is at least as urgent as that of the larger towns. Yet they cannot turn to closed circuit distribution as the answer. Need we accept in this, as in so many other things, that it's just hard luck on the rural areas?

Before long, so much money may be sunk in cable systems for the big cities that one of these days no other pattern will seem possible. Before that happens, before we become wholly committed, should we not be asking some very searching questions about alternative *broadcasting* possibilities which would make equally available to the scattered communities those advantages which we are meantime so vigorously claiming for the city systems? If we really believe that television teaching offers significant benefits to the larger towns, it is cynical to deny those benefits to the countryside schools which need them even more.

CHAPTER SEVEN

Television in the Single School

The output of the two broadcast networks is now available to schools in almost every part of the country; and a limited number of the larger cities will be adding their own closed circuit transmissions. So the television receiver should soon be a fairly normal item of classroom furniture; but how likely is it that the television camera will come to be used in the individual school? The role of the broadcasters is established; we have seen the case for the local authority system; how far can the use of television be effectively and economically decentralized?

Here, once again, the 'use of television' can mean several quite different things. It may mean employing a single camera as a perfectly straightforward visual aid. It may mean the installation of perhaps two cameras to link one classroom with another. It may also imply the more creative use of several cameras in a studio situation, to develop new forms of teaching similar to those offered by the broadcasting or larger closed circuit systems. This third possibility is the one which demands the closest examination; the other two can, respectively, be commended and rejected fairly quickly.

The single camera used as a visual aid is something that one would hope shortly to see as standard equipment, certainly in any secondary school. Its capacity to magnify detail and

84

distribute the magnified image simultaneously to many viewers has been dealt with in an earlier chapter; so there is no need at this point to offer more than a reminder of its usefulness in any field of teaching where the detailed observation of an object or an experiment is of value. Even at this utterly simple level, the television camera has much to contribute to the teaching of skills – carpentry, pottery, art, cookery, needlework, are all subjects in which it can afford the advantages of a demonstration that is virtually individual to each pupil. In biology classes, over-the-shoulder or overhead shooting of a dissection presents a picture of the whole process which is infinitely more intelligible than any other readily available method. Indeed a very wide range of laboratory activities can benefit from the enlarging eye of the television camera. Always provided that the equipment is kept simple (so that it does not demand an undue proportion of the teacher's attention) and that it is handled with as little mystique as a microscope or a slide-projector, the use of a camera in this way should before long become routine school practice.

The linking of classrooms to each other by television is quite another matter. Simple relay – as from a laboratory to a classroom – may have its uses and they certainly exist in the university context; but it is difficult to envisage many school circumstances in which this should be necessary. Nor can one feel much enthusiasm for any suggestion of 'overflow' teaching, in which lessons (presumably with some visual content) are taught direct to the class in one room and relayed by television to the pupils in another. Between 1962 and 1965 an extensive experiment in closed circuit television was carried out at Warblington County Secondary School in Hampshire [15]; and the first phase of this enquiry – a phase which lasted throughout one school year – was devoted to studying the effectiveness of a classroom-to-classroom link. Although in practice it worked, and was even considered to be effective within strict limits, the difficulties very substantially outweighed the advantages. For example, where visual material was important, its impact was reduced in the originating room because it was all visible in advance – so that television's peculiar facility for presenting the right visual image at just the right moment was immediately written off for half the audience. Since it was necessary to install monitors in the originating room as well as the remote one, there was in this respect too an unsatisfactory learning situation – a continual mental switching on the pupils' part between face-to-face conditions and the quite different attitude in which one watches a purely television presentation.

Two main considerations weigh very heavily against such a use of television within the school. First, the sheer mechanics of the business. Unless the link between any two rooms is permanently installed (and why, under ordinary school circumstances, should it be?) a quite disproportionate amount of time must be devoted to setting it up and dismantling it. Even the simplest television overflow involves a surprising amount of equipment, and if one allows for two-way sound (so that questions can be asked and answered) the complications multiply. And once all this time has been consumed, are we left with classroom conditions that are really acceptable? In the originating room, apparatus is likely to interrupt the pupils' view, there is the constant distraction of equipment which is not in itself relevant to the study in hand, while the mere presence of the pupils inhibits the mobile and most effective use of the cameras.

Second, there is almost certainly an adverse effect on the nature of the teaching. Remember that we are dealing here not with the comparatively remote lecture situation typical of much college and university work, but with schoolroom teaching which involves a much more personal and active give-and-take relationship. To confront the teacher simultaneously with two different types of audience – one class present and visible in front of him, the other remote and seeing by television alone – is to divide and distract his attention, demanding a hybrid and unsatisfactory technique. One class, or both, will suffer; for either he addresses himself to the camera and, through it, directly to the remote audience – in which case the present class

86

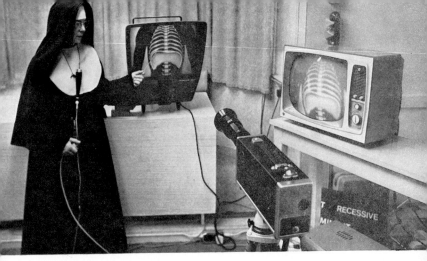

In this simple but ingenious studio, many of the usual audio-visual aids have been incorporated into television presentations. Here a film loop is being transmitted to students who receive the picture shown on the monitor at the right. Camera switching is controlled by the lecturer.

The demonstration of detail in a biology lecture. Whatever the level of study, the advantages of this purely visual-aid use of television are obvious; and, if this is all that is required, a single inexpensive camera will serve the purpose.

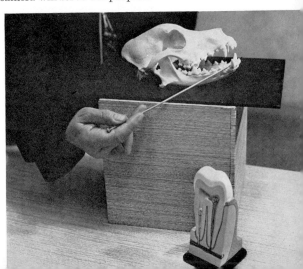

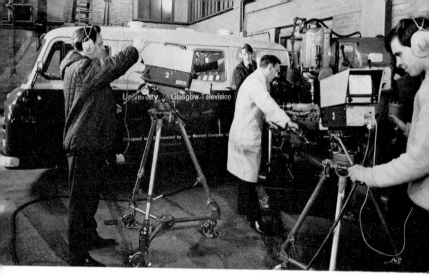

Although a mobile unit can operate with cameras quite remote from the control room, there are conditions in which the whole operation can be remarkably compact. Here, for example, the entire unit – vehicle and cameras – has moved into an engineering workshop.

The control room of Glasgow University's mobile television unit. Entirely self-contained and built into a mini-bus, this unit is used to collect recorded material in hospitals, schools, and many other points outside the University. The recordings are brought back for teaching use in the lecture-room.

become mere onlookers at a performance; or else he devotes his attention to the pupils he can see – in which case the remote class become simply eavesdroppers, denied that one-to-one contact which is possible when a teacher is free to address himself directly to the camera.

In theory, the classroom-to-classroom link has little to commend it; and in practice one cannot imagine many situations in which it would be thought desirable. At Warblington, after a year's work with television in the classroom, it was decided that all the main equipment should be moved to a studio – because of the distraction and congestion it caused in the classroom; because lighting could be more strictly controlled in a studio; and because the handling of cameras (along with all the other demands imposed by television) was proving too much of a burden on the teacher whose main function, after all, was to give a lesson.

So Warblington became one of the very few schools in this country, so far, to have its own television studio – or almost its own, since in fact it relayed its programmes to two neighbouring schools as well as to four of its own classrooms. Among other schools to carry out pioneering work in the field of single-school television were Kidbrooke Comprehensive (linked with Avery Hill College of Education) and, in Scotland, Dunfermline's Queen Anne School. Now there is a clear case in favour of the simple visual-aid use of television in the individual school: but what are we to say of the more elaborate studio set-up? When we compared the local authority systems with the national networks, we could point to the very fact of their being local as a significant advantage: but can this principle be extended indefinitely, or do we reach a stage where the educational benefits scarcely justify the financial outlay and the extra demands in staffing?

The broadcast networks and the local authority systems share, in varying degree, the capacity for wide distribution. Put every other consideration on one side, and this remains sufficient justification for their use – that they can make available to very large numbers (and, in the case of broadcasting, to a very scattered population) specialist teachers and services which would otherwise be available to only a few. The studio which serves a single school, or a small group of neighbouring schools, has at any one time an audience which is limited in size to the number of pupils on the roll within a given age group. In other words, the really major advantage of widespread distribution has disappeared; and we must therefore look very closely and critically at the remaining benefits which are claimed for the one-school studio installation.

One is forced to wonder whether many of the claims could not equally be made for *any* innovation that offered staff and pupils the opportunity of taking a fresh look at their work. The single-school system, we are told, offers the maximum degree of liaison with one's audience – in the sense, no doubt, that the teacher in the studio actually knows all the pupils to whom he is speaking remotely; but this is not so much a positive advantage as the absence of a *dis*advantage – the ultimate degree of liaison is still achieved by teaching face-to-face in the classroom. Or you will hear it argued that the preparation of a studio lesson 'stimulates new thought about teaching methods': it does, of course, and if you are forced into using television at, say, the local authority level, then it is one of the incidental benefits of the situation that there is a fresh and provocative exchange of ideas amongst all who are involved. However the important thing in any school is that there should be an exchange of ideas – the stimulus to such an exchange can be something much less expensive than a television studio.

Another standard argument is that television can 'provide teaching matter which is more quickly assimilated and more easily memorized because it is visual'; but we must not allow the enthusiasts to mislead us into imagining that television has a monopoly of the visual. Granted that one can in a studio more easily assemble a mass of heterogeneous visual material and present it in a connected and acceptable form; there remain other less expensive ways of doing this which many a teacher has never even explored. Remember that we are relating all these remarks to the resources of a single school; so that the question is not so much one of television's ability to deal with visuals (for which it has an insatiable capacity) but of the school's ability to produce them in sufficient quantity. If the end-product is to be nothing more than a lesson illustrated by occasional stills and diagrams – and there is nothing wrong with that – then it is quite possible that the blackboard, the slide projector, and adequate preparation will make just as much impact as a television lesson.

Then there is the claim that a school studio makes it possible to break down some of the subject barriers. There are, no doubt, cases in which this has been true – or at least there have been cases in which the use of the studio has made it convenient to break them down. Broadcast television, too, has long since merged geography and history, politics and economics, in programmes that deal broadly with current affairs, but it is overstating the case to suggest that television, and only television, has made this fusion possible. Once again it is simply the provision of a new stimulus, and to some extent perhaps the copying of a broadcast pattern, that has made it possible to shake subjects out of a long-established framework.

Broadcast programmes depend on a substantial team for their production, each member of that team with his own professional expertise. The city television systems realized right from the start that any one programme must result from the combined efforts of several teachers working in close co-operation. And wherever studio productions are attempted, it immediately becomes clear that only the co-ordinated work of a whole group will produce an efficient result. In the single-school studio this means the development, in effect, of a form of team-teaching: the talents of the art master and the teacher of technical subjects may well be relevant to the preparation of a history programme, and the music department need not be surprised if it is asked to make its own contribution to a programme on

G

physics. Now such exercises in team-teaching are always good for a school and its staff; and they are to be commended as a valuable by-product of television – but they must be recognized as the kind of by-product that will result from any well-designed school project, not as a justification of the television studio itself.

All this may seem to be developing into an ill-natured attack on the single-school television system, but it is not so intended. Go to any small television installation in the educational field these days, and the atmosphere will be one of hard work, open-mindedness and co-operation – without these three characteristics the studio would not be there, or would not be working. Ask about results, and you are likely to be given an account which is enthusiastic and encouraging, but which offers a confused mixture of benefits direct, indirect, and merely incidental. If we are to be objective, if we are to consider long-term developments, then from all the advantages that we claim for television we must sort out and eliminate those which we could have been seeking and achieving without it. And an objective study of the single-school television studio does suggest that, while it can contribute much that is valuable and stimulating to the life of the school, many of its benefits are incidental rather than direct.

What sort of demands does the running of a studio make upon the individual school? In terms of accommodation, it involves the sacrifice of at least one existing room or the addition of a new building. At Queen Anne School in Dunfermline, a classroom is now permanently equipped as the studio, and a smaller adjacent room has been converted into the control room. At Warblington a Terrapin building was erected and modified for use – giving a studio of 24 ft square, with a preparation room and a control room adjoining. These can be regarded as minimum requirements, since television is notoriously greedy of space – for maintenance, for the construction of even the simplest sets, and for the storage of a steadily mounting stock of spares, props, captions and stills.

To that sacrifice of space, or outlay on new building, one must add technical costs. The cabling system and the provision of monitors in the chosen reception rooms will be a relatively small expense, but the equipping of the studio itself can cost a good deal. The strictly limited distribution of the pictures within the school makes a comparatively economical system acceptable, but any sacrifice in technical quality emerges ultimately as a sacrifice in teaching quality too. The technical equipment and installation at Warblington – excluding building costs but including the link with two neighbouring schools – came to £8,275.

The demands on staffing are more difficult to specify, because – in the initial stages at any rate – they are so largely met by the enthusiasm and the after-hours work of individual teachers. But it can be assumed that a studio which is in use frequently enough to justify its existence will demand the full-time attention of at least one member of the teaching staff. At Queen Anne's in Dunfermline, Eric Holmes who originally ran the studio on a part-time basis has now been appointed its full-time director. At Warblington, after the three-year experiment during which he had been appointed full-time Head of Television Studies, P. S. Dutfield listed these as the staff required to run such a studio – studio director, assistant studio director, design director, technician, secretary, and two studio assistants. To which, of course, must be added the members of staff who actually conduct the teaching from the studio.

Mr Dutfield's list includes technical staff: a word must be added about the particular importance of their role. Whenever television is used at anything more than the simplest visual-aid level, there is always the danger that the sheer mechanical operation of the equipment may claim more of a teacher's attention than the content of his teaching. At Warblington, as elsewhere, this was discovered in the early stages – 'Much out of the school time was spent studying the workings of the equipment and it became increasingly clear that this was a role for the specialist. If closed-circuit television was to be applied to education, then the role of the teacher should be to make use of the equipment rather than make it work.' So we must include in our staffing requirements at least one well-qualified technician: he will rapidly prove himself to be the most indispensable member of the team.

Recollect now that Glasgow's city-wide system, catering for 315 schools and colleges, got off the ground with a full-time staff numbering only ten; cast your eye again over Mr Dutfield's estimate of requirements (which is not an exaggerated one); and ask yourself whether the single-school system can really be justified in economic terms.

If we consider its strictly teaching role alone, it is a little difficult to see just where the single-school studio fits in. Once again, this is not to criticize nor discount the work that has already been done in individual schools: but one must ask whether, as a *type*, the mini-system has a distinctive contribution to make. Enrichment programmes, in the generally accepted sense of the term, are obviously beyond its technical and financial resources – they are unlikely to be tackled even by the bigger local authority services. Heavily illustrated lessons – on the history of art, for example, or on some aspects of geography – can be neatly handled by television, but meantime without the advantages of colour which can be supplied by film or the slide-projector. In some cases one finds an emphasis on discussion programmes with perhaps a local notability taking part, but is this not an irrational carry-over from broadcast television? We have discussions and extended interviews on the networks because only thus can the distinguished speakers be made available in millions of homes: but if the editor of the local paper is in our school and prepared to discuss the freedom of the press, can we not see and hear him more effectively in the flesh in the school hall?

Is it for direct teaching, then, that the school's own television unit should be used? As we have seen, the broadcasters are moving towards direct teaching; and its provision is one explicit purpose of the city systems; grudgingly or otherwise we are all beginning to admit that this is a need which television can meet.

But it is a need that we only consider to exist when the number of teachers (or specialists) available is quite inadequate in relation to the teaching that has to be done. Very few would go so far as to suggest that direct teaching can be better achieved by television than in a face-to-face situation. So within any individual school which has a staff that can afford all the extra time that television demands, it is difficult to see why a direct lesson by television should ever seem preferable to the same lesson given in the classroom.

Nevertheless perhaps there is a case for the single-school system which in fact serves several other schools as well, as in the Warblington experiment. This could certainly have the virtue of sharing the teaching load among the specialist teachers available in the group, and in many respects the advantages claimed for the local authority system might be mirrored on a smaller scale. However the disadvantages would be there too; and the final report on Warblington echoes some of them – 'The obstacles to the useful operation of such a link are the lack of curriculum standardization and time-table uniformity and the problem of co-ordination between traditionally independent institutions. Unless these difficulties can be overcome, the advantages of small scale working are marginal and cannot justify the expenditure of money, time and effort.'

No mention has been made so far of one item which can make a substantial difference to the usefulness of television within the single-school – the videotape recording machine. We have spoken as though any television activity in the school, whether it be a one-camera demonstration or a more elaborate studio production, must be carried out live, seen once and for all, and finished with. However portable videotape recorders of several types are now available and, if the extra money can be found to purchase one, its existence will more than double the usefulness of any television equipment that is already held. At the simplest level a one-camera demonstration, using perhaps scarce or perishable material, can be recorded and used repeatedly. In the case of more elaborate presentations, such as one might prepare in a school studio, the use of videotape makes it reasonable to devote more time and expense to a programme that can be used without further preparation over a number of years. It may even be that the use of VTRs will make it more realistically possible for small groups of schools to co-operate in the use of television by distributing recordings on tape rather than sending programmes live by cable.

In general, however – and even allowing for the greater freedom and long-term economy that videotape permits – one has to express doubts about the viability of the single-school studio. Television at the studio level of organization requires a very considerable concentration of resources. It demands accommodation; it depends on expensive equipment that needs constant maintenance and costly replacements such as camera tubes; it requires its own permanent staff. Even with that permanent staff, the success of a school studio must rest largely on the enthusiasm and the voluntary co-operation of the subject teachers: only a guaranteed and long-term enthusiasm can justify the large investment that even a small studio represents.

CHAPTER EIGHT

Television in Teacher Training

Television is contributing to the total educational process at many points today; but there can be few areas in which its potential, direct and indirect, is demonstrated more strikingly than in the colleges of education. Here, the camera offers completely new dimensions to the quality of training that students can be given in their own professional skills; here, too, familiarity with the electronic tools of their trade can gradually build up in a new generation of teachers the fresh attitudes that are necessary if television and radio are to be accepted as quite normal, indeed basic, means of instruction. In schools, in universities, and in adult education generally, one could reasonably say that what matters most is the nature of the teaching material conveyed by television; the end-product and its effect are the things that interest us. The college of education, however, must nowadays be concerned not merely with the best ways of teaching students *through* television, but with offering instruction in the actual techniques of television itself. Let us begin at the beginning – which, in the case of teacher training, means that we look first at class observation.

Most of us who have been trained as teachers can recollect the dreary hours we spent sitting behind a class of children – or perhaps, with even greater embarrassment, sitting in front of them – dutifully 'observing'. That, at least, was the professed purpose of our visit. Just what we should be observing was not always clear to us, and the activities in the classroom often seemed to bear only a remote and limited resemblance to those envisaged in the teaching theory which had been expounded to us in the college. The luck of the draw, we suspected, must have landed us with a singularly incapable teacher, for surely we could have done better ourselves; alternatively, things went so well and so easily that there must, we felt, be a lot of unnecessary fuss about this business of teaching methods. In short, the periods of observation endured by the student teacher were – and no doubt still are – often singularly unprofitable. They were unprofitable because they were undirected. Such commentary as we were given on teaching method was in general terms, related of necessity to generalized and hypothetical cases; sometimes, it seemed, almost wilfully unrelated to the real life of the classrooms we were observing.

To this whole situation – which is, after all, absolutely central to the process of teacher training – television has brought the opportunity of quite startling change and improvement. Basically the possibility is this: in the classroom you install a few cameras – normally two or three will be sufficient, though some colleges use more – and their pictures are fed out by cable to a remote room in which the classroom activities can be observed in considerable detail by as many students as need to watch. This basic pattern can, of course, be modified in various ways. It may be thought preferable to set aside a room in the college as a studio-classroom, in which case the pupils are brought to the college and it is a simple matter to relay the whole lesson to an observation room elsewhere in the same building. Alternatively, it may be possible to install a cable or microwave link between a demonstration school and the college, in which case the teacher and the pupils – still in their own accustomed classroom – can be observed more remotely but equally effectively. A third alternative is that, within the school itself, the demonstration lesson is recorded on a portable videotape machine, and the recording can be viewed subsequently in the college. The relative advantages of each method can be discussed later; the really substantial benefits become available whichever method is used. What are these benefits?

For a start, the student teacher is no longer placed disadvantageously at the back of the classroom, no longer anchored to the one spot where he is least able to observe all the subtle interplay of stimulus and reaction that go to make up the teaching and learning process. Through the several cameras that have been brought to bear upon the situation, he has at once a wider and a more detailed view of the class and its activities than is available to any single observer in the room. In this sense he has an advantage over the teacher who is giving the lesson – he has access to even more information about what is going on in the room, and can study in detail the reactions which at any one moment seem to be most significant. In practice, of course, the student does not see the pictures offered by all the cameras : he sees the one picture which from moment to moment is selected for him. This need not be considered a handicap : the unpractised eye, presented simultaneously with three or four television pictures of the same activity, is not enlightened but distracted and bemused. It is to the student's considerable advantage that the output of all the classroom cameras can be directed, shaped and selected by the lecturer-producer who is in charge. This indeed is the really significant part of the operation : it is this selection, this underlining of the aspects that matter, that makes the television relay so effective an alternative to the generalized, puzzled and undirected observation of the inexperienced student.

That this makes for the better training of the student teacher is doubtless the main consideration, but one cannot ignore in passing the considerable administrative advantages of the new situation. The allocation of students for observation periods has always been a problem, and with increasing numbers it has become even more acute. Not every practising teacher offers good material for the beginner's instruction ; and there must have been wide variations in the quality and usefulness of the work offered to students as a model for their own early teaching practice. At one stroke, television offers a solution to several of these related problems. It can substantially reduce the burden on the schools and on the individual teacher, since one lesson can be observed by literally hundreds of students. It can eliminate a large amount of wasted travelling time between school and college, and it can ensure that the teaching offered to the student for observation is, for training purposes, the most appropriate.

This last is an important point. What, for training purposes, is it most appropriate to offer? One is tempted to assume automatically that only the best teaching should be offered, that students should not in their inexperience be exposed to indifferent or poor standards of performance. If their observation has to be carried out alone and subjectively, if the teaching they have seen cannot in the nature of things be submitted to the comment and analysis of an expert, then they should – ideally – study only those practices which they can with advantage imitate. But television affects this situation too: for now the methods lecturer observes along with his students, he sees what they see, and he can simultaneously or retrospectively add his own commentary – a commentary which will draw attention to questions of technique, to the points at which a lesson took the right or the wrong turning. In other words, remote observation (because it makes possible the addition of expert analytical comment) considerably widens the range and quality of teaching to which students can safely, indeed profitably, be exposed.

The use of videotape recording, in this as in so many other contexts, adds considerably to the value of television observation. There is the obvious initial advantage that any one teaching presentation can be shown repeatedly to different classes, thus reducing still further the demands made upon the schools. Where a recording is seen to be suitable for the purpose, it can be used as the basis of a study to which the lecturers from several different departments can contribute – the methods lecturer, the psychologist, the subject specialist, the educational theorist. The lecturer may well find it rewarding to study the recording himself before showing it to his students, so that they can be alerted in advance to the particular developments they should watch for. Another possibility is that the recording may be edited, streamlined, or used in the form of excerpts to illustrate the main points of a lecture. Or again there will often be value in viewing a lesson, discussing its effectiveness with the class, then viewing parts of it for a second time in the light of the points that have been raised in discussion.

Whether recorded or not, remote observation of a class by television offers this fundamental advantage – that the whole group of students, and their lecturer, share the same experience. Their discussion can now be based on common ground, not on a variety of individually recollected fragments and subjective judgments that are based on widely different observations of classroom behaviour. Theory can thus be related much more directly to practice: it can no longer shelter behind the hypothetical instance, but must show itself to be capable of application to the real-life situation which is presented to them all simultaneously.

Though classroom observation by television will be useful at all school stages, one should mention its particular value in the study of very young children. Here the intrusion of students in a group of any size can be especially distracting, and any less obtrusive form of surveillance is to be welcomed. The use of cameras for the study of infant-room behaviour in unstructured groups is not without its technical problems, for it is a rapidly changing and unpredictable set of circumstances that one attempts to cover; but of the various alternative possibilities that are available, television observation seems to be clearly the most promising.

It is perhaps appropriate at this point to add a word about the control, the production, of classroom observation by television. As has already been pointed out, there must be an element of selection before the chosen picture reaches the students; and it is immaterial whether the selection is made from two, or four, or six alternative sources – the choice of shot is still a significant one. Do we at any given moment show the teacher or the class, a wide-angle picture of the whole room or the close-up of an individual reaction? The choices are innumerable, and may have to be made in a split second. The over-riding consideration must, of course, be the professional purpose for which the cameras are being used: if our intention is to offer an effective account of the lesson and of pupils' reactions to it, that intention will condition every choice. As any television director knows, however, it is possible – by choosing this shot or that – to give two quite different accounts of one and the same situation. Now within the college context all this adds up to one quite obvious requirement – that the man who is directing the cameras and choosing the shots should be someone who knows what he is looking for, not merely in terms of television but even more clearly in terms of teaching. To the classroom lesson that is being relayed he must be capable of adding another level of teaching, the level that adds rapidly selected but appropriate visual comment. This is a new dimension in teaching, and its effective realization depends on all the skills of the conventional lecturer plus concentration, a capacity for quick and firm decisions, and a clear appreciation of the precise purpose for which any one television transmission is being made. Without the exercise of such abilities, a great part of television's contribution to this aspect of teacher training would be lost.

One or two technical and organizational problems should be briefly mentioned. Since sound radio has been with us so much longer than television, the layman is apt to imagine that visual coverage is a more complex affair than sound coverage; and in the purchase of equipment one is apt to devote any amount of attention to cameras and their qualities, but very little to the characteristics of the microphone. In practice, however, it is the effective relay of sound that causes most of the problems in classroom observation – particularly in active and mobile situations such as one encounters with the younger age groups. Expert advice should therefore be sought on the acoustic treatment of rooms where observation is to be carried out, and one should be prepared for a good deal of experiment before settling on the types of microphone most suitable for this work.

Should the cameras we use for observation be remotely controlled, or can we use cameramen without disrupting the work of the class? Both methods have been successfully employed, and both have their protagonists. In theory, the remotely controlled camera should prove less intrusive; but it offers two disadvantages – one, that some types of remote control gear are noisy in operation and thus cause distraction at the very moments when we especially wish to avoid it; the other, that their movements are relatively slow, so that we may miss the quick reaction shot which can be so telling. Those of us who have used manned cameras in the classroom find that the cameramen are – with most age groups, and particularly with younger children – very soon accepted and forgotten. The manually controlled camera, of course, offers much greater mobility and quick response to direction; and an intelligent cameraman who is in sympathy with his director can be of the greatest help in offering shots which are likely to make a significant contribution to the interpretation of the situation.

As we indicated at the outset, class observations may be carried out within a college studio or in the school to which the pupils belong. Local circumstances will often settle this issue; but on balance one feels that the most realistic results are likely to be obtained in the atmosphere to which the pupils are accustomed. Their usual classroom conditions may indeed be a factor relevant to their whole attitude, and it would be a pity if observation were to be conducted under circumstances which were doubly artificial, both the surroundings and the cameras providing their quota of distraction. Because it is so desirable that a class should be seen in its normal setting, colleges are likely to see the need for a mobile television unit which – if videotape is included in its facilities, as it certainly should be –

can collect material from a wide range of schools, including those which offer subjects for special study like remedial teaching, speech training, language laboratories, or facilities for the handicapped child.

Let us turn now to a different aspect of observation: this time the observation of the student himself. Though he will learn from the study of other people's teaching techniques, he must also practise his own; and here the use of videotape again offers new possibilities – essentially, the opportunity of self-assessment in conjunction with the constructive criticism of a methods lecturer.

This is an exercise which may take varying forms: in one United States university it has emerged as 'micro-teaching', and this is how Professor Stanley Donner of Stanford University describes it:

Micro-teaching is really a scaled down teaching situation; scaled down in both class size and in time. The practice teacher will meet a class of one to five students and teach from five to twenty minutes. Micro-teaching lends itself to all kinds of controls for the level of teaching, the subject matter, and the classroom circumstances can be arranged in advance. The logistics of practice teaching are of course vastly simplified and the supervising instructor can focus his efforts on the particular points he wishes his practice teacher to learn. A television videotape recording is made of the lesson, the practice teacher will review his tape, receive student evaluations of his teaching, review the lesson with his supervisor and reteach his lesson to a new group of students to see what improvement he can make [16].

Research at Stanford has shown that success in micro-teaching and successful teaching in the normal classroom situation are highly correlated. One can envisage several variations of this technique, depending on the amount of time and the technical facilities available; one way or another, it should not be overlooked.

However, teaching practice and class observation are not the whole story of our colleges of education, nor are they the only aspects of teacher training to be touched by television. Within the next few years we can expect to find that some fifty or sixty of these colleges in Britain will be making regular use of television, and many of them will have their own studio. Where local authority systems exist, there will normally be a cable link between the central school studio and the colleges: such a link already operates between the Glasgow system and Jordanhill College, and similar arrangements are planned by the Inner London Education Authority. A valuable two-way traffic should develop between the schools and the colleges. Student teachers, on the one hand, will add to their observation of the conventional classroom situation the study of teaching techniques that have been adapted for direct teaching by television; meantime the colleges will have acquired a new channel through which to offer in-service training to teachers in school.

However the most fruitful use of the television studio should develop within the college itself. As in the universities, it will no doubt be found that certain areas of college teaching can be more effectively dealt with from the studio; and this should in its own way be useful as training for the students in their own later use of television lessons in the classroom. It is very much to be hoped that the purpose which the college studio will mainly serve is the training of students in television techniques. Though this may at first sight seem a surprising view, there are at least three good reasons why training in television should be the priority. Of these, the first and most strictly practical reason is that the local authority television systems will create an increasing demand. There will be a demand for teachers who can write scripts, direct, and teach to the camera: three quite different skills, but they must all be based on a sound working knowledge of the whole television process. Trial and error methods, learning by experience, are all very well for the earliest days of an experimental enterprise; but we are past the experimental stage now, we know that local systems are viable and will multiply, and this new aspect of teaching should be catered for systematically within the profession. But the demand that will be created by the local services includes another element. Only a small proportion of teachers will, after all, actively participate at the studio end of the operation. The much wider need will be for a body of teachers in the classrooms, at the receiving end, who have sufficient understanding of the medium to offer informed and constructive criticism of the programmes that are transmitted – people who can tell you not simply that they thought a lesson was ineffective, but can explain in both teaching and television terms why it was ineffective.

The second reason for giving the student teacher a training in television techniques has wider implications. Not every teacher will work in one of the big cities, or become involved in its television system, but for the great majority of teachers broadcast television programmes do offer a source of matériel that is often used to less than its full advantage. And part of the reason for this is that the teacher and the broadcaster, by professional upbringing, tend to think, communicate, and teach in fundamentally different styles. The teacher (and here we are generalizing, of course) starts from first principles and proceeds in words, and with the help of the printed page, to develop his theme logically from stage to stage. We are inclined to teach as we were taught, and why should he do otherwise? The broadcaster on the other hand (even though, as a schools producer, he was originally a teacher himself) works in a different atmosphere. His weapon is the image rather than the word; he is more likely to offer you an experience than a closely developed argument; and when he directs your attention to a book, he usually hopes that you will study it later, not now. In their different ways, both methods work. The trouble is that many teachers feel themselves puzzled by the broadcast method, out of sympathy with it: surely it is all rather superficial? But, given the chance, children seem to understand it all much better than their teachers do. Now here is the point: if broadcast programmes are to be viewed – and followed up by effective discussion and development – in the school, the teacher must be capable of watching the programmes at the same level, on the same wavelength if one may put it that way, as the children themselves. And it is infinitely more likely that he will achieve this sympathy with the television approach if he has himself gained some working knowledge, however rudimentary, of the principles and the practical considerations upon which that approach is based.

There is a third and most cogent reason why the colleges of education should use their studios for the study of television itself. We have been strangely slow, in this country, about the sharpening of our critical faculties on the two most potent means of communication we possess – radio and television. In schools and universities, we devote plenty of time to literary analysis and criticism; we take to pieces the works of Scott and Hardy, contrast the styles and motive of this poet with that. We turn our attention (though still in a literary way) to drama, and make sure that every schoolboy knows why Shakespeare introduced the drunken porter in *Macbeth*. Our motives, of course, are of the best: we are determined that our children shall be able to distinguish the good from the bad, the emotional from the sentimental, the artistic from the grandiose. There is nothing wrong with the motives, but we must extend the field to which our critical faculties are applied. The impact of television on the average citizen these days is at least as great as that of literature, infinitely greater than that of the live theatre. Television programmes influence his attitude to religion, to politics and international affairs; more questionably, they may even affect his own moral judgments. Yet in the matter of television criticism we are largely casual and uninformed; we are aware of television's influence, but vague about the means by which it is exerted; and as educationists we are doing little to change the situation.

Let it be clearly understood that it is criticism at a practical level that we are speaking about, not the vapourings of the long-haired intellectual. Television is used to influence opinion – there need be no sinister implication in this: but, if you prefer it, say simply that television depends, very broadly, on two elements – the spoken word, and the visual image. The manipulation of these two, in coincidence or in juxtaposition, can result in materially different accounts of any given situation. Take the simplest sort of example. A politician, let us say, is being questioned by a professional interviewer; and in reply to an apparently straightforward question he gives a quite categorical answer. As he answers, we may be given a close shot of his face, and his expression has that patent sincerity which is the stock-in-trade of many a politician. We do not doubt the truth of what he says. On the other hand, while we *hear* his answer we may *see* a close shot of the interviewer looking politely incredulous. This time our tendency is perhaps to take his answer with a pinch of salt. A third possibility – not likely to be considered such 'good television' – is that throughout the answer we can see both politician and interviewer, in which case we are left rather more to draw our own conclusions, though even here the exact angle of the shot can favour one speaker's credibility rather than the other's.

Now this hypothetical instance must not be sensationally misinterpreted. Television producers and directors do not spend their evenings consciously slanting the truth this way or that: but they can present the whole truth only so far as television allows them to. Take this utterly simple example merely as demonstrating the kind of basic technique of which we should, as viewers, be intelligently aware. Contrary to popular belief, television does not give us the whole picture: it gives a highly selective account of proceedings, and we should be able to judge whether the selection is being made well or badly.

To elaborate a little on this theme let us pursue the same imaginary politician. He has had a long day in the House, he is in the middle of delicate negotiations, he is tired, and he is watching the clock because he has to be back at Westminster in time for a division. Is it legitimate to borrow a dramatic technique and shoot him in such detailed close-up that every flicker of his eyelid seems to carry some significance? Or is it an unwarrantable intrusion amounting to a distortion of the facts by visual manipulation? We need not agree on the answer; the important thing is to be aware of the techniques by which opinion – our opinion – is being influenced.

Or take the whole question of illustration. When does a picture genuinely add to one's understanding? When should a picture be allowed to speak for itself because the spoken word would be superfluous and distracting? When does the use of illustrative material become excessive and insulting to the intelligent viewer? These and a dozen other questions of their kind should be somewhere at the back of our minds when we are watching television; they are of at least as much importance to us in our everyday viewing as are the principles of literary criticism to our lesiure reading. It is at this practical level that our student teachers should be encouraged to develop their critical approach to television.

We can make a start by giving them a grounding in studio techniques. Teachers who have practised these techniques themselves will be more alive to the significance and potential of broadcasting generally. They are likely to practise, and to stimulate in their pupils, an attitude of healthy criticism to television and radio which is the only sure recipe for maintaining in this country the enviably high standards of broadcasting which we have so far enjoyed.

CHAPTER NINE

Television in the Universities

In the spring of 1965, a visitor to Britain from the Netherlands – he was carrying out an enquiry for the Council of Europe – was quoted thus in the *Times Educational Supplement:* 'I am trying to find out which universities in the United Kingdom are using television. Can you tell me if there is a list, or who would know about it?' His bewilderment was not surprising – there was no list; and, although television had in fact been used in at least one medical school as early as 1958, such developments as there were had usually taken place on a departmental basis, often without the knowledge even of other departments in the same university. In the last few years, however, there has been a very considerable upsurge of television activity in the universities, with a much more general exchange of information. The lines along which television services may most usefully be organized intra-murally were sketched out in the Brynmor Jones Report [17] which appeared at the end of 1965. A year later, the Research Unit of the National Extension College produced a report called 'University Intercommunication'[18] which surveys the television situation as it exists in British universities at the moment, and examines in particular the possibilities of developing an interchange of teaching material – live or recorded – between one university and another.

108

Only in the form of a catalogue could one hope to present a complete picture of the current spread of activities. The purposes, and the technical and professional standards at which television teaching is being produced, are various in the extreme. The departmental organization of resources is still the general rule. To pick a few examples, completely at random – Sheffield makes use of television in physiology and biochemistry; in University College, electrical engineering has pioneered its use; in Birmingham half a dozen departments have been using it independently; Bristol has cameras in radiology and zoology. The list could go on and on; but it would mean very little, since the 'use of television' in one place may indicate merely that a camera has been attached to an X-ray image intensifier, whilst in another it implies a near-studio level of complexity.

The Brynmor Jones Report (which, although it was nominally confined to higher scientific education, really dealt with university work in general) recommended that universities should establish central units to cover 'the whole field of communication'; such units would have responsibilities for television, film, still photography, the entire range of audio-visual material. In the longer-established universities such a re-grouping of activities is likely to take some time, even where the idea proves acceptable; but in the University of Sussex there now exists a Centre for Academic Services which closely follows the Brynmor Jones proposal, and which of course includes the provision of television facilities among its functions. Meantime a few universities had – so far as television was concerned – anticipated the central unit idea. The University of Strathclyde led the way with a permanent studio whose services were available to all departments; while the Universities of Leeds and Glasgow – after some preliminary experiments in both cases – were the first to appoint full-time professional Directors of Television, both of whom left the BBC to start this new work in March of 1965. Since that time several other universities have set up, or announced plans for, similar centralized university television services; and it seems probable that, on the grounds of both

109

effectiveness and economy, this will become the normal pattern.

A first-hand account is usually worth any amount of hearsay, generalization and theory; so perhaps it will not be considered immodest if our survey of university television is, substantially, an account of its development in the University of Glasgow. Written from this point of view, it may be all the more useful to others who are contemplating the same kind of service.

It was in 1963 that a few members of the teaching staff suggested that the university should consider what television might have to offer. It was decided, wisely, to experiment on a small scale first; and two simple but sturdy cameras were purchased with a selection of lenses, a small amount of lighting, and a couple of monitors. That was all. Except, of course, for the most important point – which was that the university also appointed a technician whose sole responsibility was the maintenance of this equipment and its operation in a whole variety of experimental situations. Right from the start, then, there was someone whose only concern was television; and it was either a happy accident or a far-sighted bit of planning that this principle was established at the very beginning.

For eighteen months or so these cameras led a varied existence: they were tried out in biochemistry and geography, in electrical engineering and modern history, in the veterinary school and in art lectures for the extra-mural department. By that time a sufficient number of people were convinced that television did have something to offer, and the university decided that it was time to go ahead on a bigger scale. It was agreed that television should be established as a central service – that is, as a facility operating separately and professionally as television, and available to whichever teaching departments wished to use it. This decision seemed to be justified on two counts – first, that it was sound economically, since it would ensure the maximum use of expensive equipment; second, that in both its operation and its direction the equipment would be handled by

110

people whose business was television, so that what was designed as a new facility would not become simply an extra burden on staff whose energies and attention were already fully committed in teaching.

So the university's television service came into being, with a director, one technician, a secretary; and of course two cameras. It seemed important that television should not arrive on the scene as something that would glibly superimpose on established university conventions a pattern wholly dictated by the new medium. One must equip: but for what? People kept asking what kind of programmes we intended to produce: but it did not follow that 'programmes' were what the teaching staff had in mind. The provision of a studio might seem to be a reasonable starting point: yet were there existing demands which made a studio absolutely necessary? Obviously the first job was to discover in some detail what the teaching departments – close on a hundred of them – really wanted in the way of television. Many of them, understandably enough, wanted nothing. Many others were quite prepared to consider any ideas that we might have to offer, but admitted to feeling no pressing need for our services. We could return to them in the course of time, but the first priority seemed to be that group of departments which already had quite clearly defined requirements. And none of these, at the time of our original enquiry, were requirements which demanded a studio or involved anything like a 'programme' in the broadcast sense.

The demands fell into two fairly clear groups. First there were those who urgently needed television as a visual aid in the quite literal sense. They wanted it in a large variety of situations which shared the same principle that we have already discussed in general terms and in the context of school work – that within a laboratory or classroom, or perhaps within a couple of neighbouring rooms, anything up to five hundred students should be able to see what would otherwise be visible to perhaps half a dozen. The second group had quite different requirements. Mobility was the characteristic they demanded – freedom to go outside the university and bring back as recordings the material to which they could not transport a whole class of students. Nor was this desire for mobility confined to any one faculty: the medical staff wanted it so that they could collect material in a variety of specialist hospitals; the social researchers saw it as a way of lecturing about planning problems actually out on site; the educationists wanted it so that (like their colleagues in the college of education) they could collect material in the school classroom and language laboratory.

The early stages of development, then, were clearly outlined by the nature of the demand. We had to provide adequate and appropriate cameras to cover the straightforward need for television as a visual aid; and we had to evolve rapidly some sort of mobile unit sophisticated enough to cover a wide range of requirements, small enough to gain easy access to odd corners of the university and teaching hospitals, self-contained enough to make minimum demands on accommodation wherever we went, and cheap enough to be an acceptable proposition.

To meet the visual-aid demand was fairly simple: the difficulty was to assess the exact amount of equipment we needed, keeping economy in mind on the one hand, and on the other allowing for the time-table peaks that build up in any university. In practice we began this side of our work – we call it the 'central pool' – with six cameras, two with viewfinders, two without. We have added another two, and the demand suggests that further additions cannot long be postponed. There may be surprise that the number is so small; but these cameras work hard. A camera can be regarded as resting if it has only one assignment in the day; it is behaving fairly normally if it has two quite different jobs morning and afternoon; and evening work is far from rare. The good sense of operating television as a central service is showing itself in maximum utilization of equipment. However it seemed, even in the early stages, that it would be wasteful to have all these cameras capable of operating only as single chains. For one thing, there were many cases in which one camera could just do the job but where two would be infinitely

112

more effective. For another, it seemed likely that one mobile unit, even when we got it, could not always meet the demand for more elaborate undertakings. So we got the ancillary equipment which made it possible to assemble any three of the central pool cameras and work them together as a unit. We evolved a small completely portable desk for sound and vision mixing; and we acquired a van to do all the fetching and carrying. That was the stage we had reached by the beginning of our first operational session in the autumn of 1965.

Our coverage of the mobile requirements was taking a little longer to plan. Just as it made sense that our central pool cameras should be capable of forming a scratch unit when necessary, so there was a strong case for getting a mobile unit which could, for some time at least, tackle the kind of job for which studio equipment would normally be considered necessary. A studio would come, but meantime it was clear that it need not be a top priority: nevertheless it was reasonable to assume (and events have proved us right) that, once people started to use television at all, their ideas would rapidly become more elaborate. Departmental requests had indicated a good many undertakings that would certainly need three cameras. Once they got the hang of things, they would want caption material in plenty: should we be prepared frequently to lose one of our three cameras on caption work, or should we add a caption scanner as well? We did; so our mobile unit has in fact four cameras – all vidicons, three of them with viewfinders and available for normal operation, the fourth in the caption scanner.

Everything within reason was done to save space and streamline our operation. The unit has been built into a mini-bus which houses a complete control room in miniature – it is operated by a director and one engineer. The caption scanner is fitted with variable lighting which enables it to take either transparencies or opaque captions; and when the need arises it operates with a zoom lens so that not all the illustrative material need be of standard size or specially prepared for television. Between the vision desk and the sound desk is a small panel controlling a

113

sound feedback system through which, if the unit is being used for overflow purposes, students at up to three remote points can put their questions to the lecturer. A portable videotape recorder travels as part of the unit, and cabling is sufficient for the cameras to operate at a distance of five hundred feet away from the van.

With all this, of course, came increases in staff. There are over a dozen of us now, including a producer, an assistant, a technical supervisor and five technicians. A graphics artist looks after the demand for caption material which did develop as we had envisaged, and there are two driver-handymen. What sort of work have they all been making possible?

The equipment intended primarily for visual aid has been tackling a larger range of work than that description might be taken as implying. First, the obvious types of use. In pathology, one camera is regularly used in the autopsy room to demonstrate post mortem material to undergraduates. Here the problem is one of ensuring that the whole class can be given a clear view of specimens which are perishable and difficult to handle; the changes to which their attention must be drawn are of many types, often slight and on a very small scale; with other methods of demonstration, many students have been unable to see in anything like sufficient detail. The great lack here is colour – we are, of course, operating as yet with black-and-white only – but the significant thing is, that in spite of this restriction, television continues to be thought worth employing.

Agricultural botany provides another example of visual-aid use. Here an overhead camera is used to relay around the laboratory the detail of plant dissections. The time taken to cover such demonstration work has been reduced by 20 per cent; material which is in short supply – quite often there may be only one good specimen of a type available – can be used for a large class; and student reactions are very favourable. One drawback reported by the staff is that the quality of their own work, thus observed, has to be of a higher standard than previously.

Still within the strictly visual-aid field, but using two or three of these cameras, we regularly cover much more elaborate demonstration work, notably in subjects like chemistry and physics where it is important that students should at an early stage in their course be given expert and detailed instruction in points of experimental technique. With classes numbering around five hundred, as they do, television has offered particular advantages; not only because of the detail it displays but also because videorecording and repeated reproductions have so substantially reduced the amount of time spent by teaching staff on the setting-up and demonstration of elaborate experiments. (The time thus saved has, incidentally, been devoted to the development of small discussion group teaching.) Prepared in the laboratory, where the demonstrations would normally be carried out, the videotape recordings are subsequently played into a lecture theatre, where they become simply an illustrated part of the lecture, very much as models or wall-charts might be used.

Perhaps one should pause here for a moment to make one or two general points that arise from this type of work. First, that quite apart from the ultimate saving in time for teaching staff – because one recording provides many repeat performances – there is often a saving in time within the showing of the experiment itself; where the experiment involves the frequent but inevitable repetition of a process or a measurement, the merely repetitive element can be cut out. One thinks, for example, of a physics experiment which takes nearly three hours of laboratory time: recorded and telescoped, it can be shown as completely as necessary in forty minutes. Where large classes are of necessity divided up into smaller groups for demonstration and tutorial purposes, the recording of experiments brings another advantage – that every smaller group is known to have had exactly the same teaching; that one knows the demonstration has been properly and successfully carried out, free of the minor blemishes and mishaps that can so often invalidate the live performance. But why, one may ask, use television and videotape for such

115

demonstration work at all when in many cases films of a similar order exist? Because, our teaching staff tell us, films of this kind suffer from too readily becoming permanent; they become dated, and departmental ideas on teaching can diverge considerably from their content. With videotape, on the other hand, teaching material can be put together using the department's own equipment and personnel: students are thus given details that are wholly relevant to the course as it is at present being run, and are taught throughout and consistently by their own teachers. As any one tape becomes outdated because of changes in ideas or in staff, it is an inexpensive and simple matter to erase it and make a new recording.

One could considerably extend the list of subjects in which the cameras have offered this more elaborate form of visual aid – in veterinary pharmacology, biochemistry, radiology and a variety of medical departments – but in all these cases the principles and the advantages remain substantially the same. So let us look at another application of our work – the overflow lecture. With many other universities we share the problem of classes which have grown in size beyond the limits of existing lecture-room accommodation. Our cameras have in some departments eased the situation by relaying the proceedings to a second lecture theatre. Few of us, probably, would feel that this is the most desirable way of employing one's television resources; yet it is a practical proposition, and in our own experience has worked remarkably well. Individual lecturer's reactions to the idea vary widely; some resent the extra lighting that is necessary, others adjust to it very quickly; some are acutely conscious of the remote audience and feel they have to cater specially for it, while others find it easier to concentrate on the present audience and trust the television staff to cater adequately for the rest. Others again, after some experience of the overflow method, decide that the best solution is to dispense with this hybrid technique and declare their preference for lecturing straight to the camera in a studio setting. What matters rather more, however, is the effectiveness with which the overflow lecture reaches the students in the remote room. Assuming that the lecture is quite simply talk-and-chalk (which it very often is), how much is lost by the remote audience? So far as this country is concerned, we cannot yet claim to have established a dependable answer to that question. American evidence, of course, suggests that remarkably little is lost; and without statistics to back us up, we in Glasgow would say the same. Student reactions at the receiving end are indistinguishable from those in the originating room; they laugh, and hiss, and scrape their feet, and pay attention, in just the same ways as those who are sitting in front of their lecturer. In other words, they give no indication that they feel themselves to be undergoing an experience markedly different from that of the ordinary lecture room. Student opinion on the matter is not uniform; a very few resent the fact that they are no longer entirely free to manipulate their own attention – they can look at the blackboard only when the television director presents it to them; but the fact of the matter is that, given freedom of choice, rather more sit in the television room than in the live lecture room. For this, of course, the cynic could advance a variety of reasons. Immediate colleagues, reporting on each other's performances, characteristically comment that they are, on television, 'more impressive than in the flesh'.

What does emerge from our own short experience of the technique is that there is much more involved in the effective relay of a lecture than simply locking off the cameras on a wide-angle shot and pumping the pictures through. Well directed, the cameras can largely compensate for anything the student loses by not being in direct personal contact with the lecturer; they can eliminate some of his more distracting mannerisms; and the manipulation of the remote student's attention between lecturer, blackboard and other demonstration material can (even if a few initially resent it) be constructive. All this does imply that the cameras are directed by someone who is in essence an educator rather than a showman: he must be capable of thinking himself into the student situation and presenting at any one

117

moment the shot which most students will be anxious to have
– one can, for example, have very good reason to cut away to a
calculation that is on the blackboard even though the lecturer is
not meantime explicitly pointing it out. In short, this apparently
routine and rather dull form of television activity calls for a
considerable degree of thought and responsibility.

The overflow lecture, of course, is simply one example of
television's capacity to relay. This capacity we have used in a
number of more obviously creative ways: for example in the relay of interviews – psychological, medical, psychiatric. Assemble
a large audience of students around a patient, and you are
unlikely to find him at his best or his most natural. Place him
in a room with a one-way screen and he may feel more relaxed;
it is your students who are now at an added disadvantage. But
let the doctor interview the patient in the most normal setting
for such a talk (in his office, or in a side-room off the ward) and
relay the result to as large a lecture theatre as you like, or as
many seminar rooms. Each student is then individually, as it
were, sitting beside the patient – able to see the most detailed
view of every mannerism, every visible symptom that may be of
significance. Here television is beginning to operate in some real
sense as television; because, whereas with the older methods
there had somehow to be superimposed on the interview a commentary that would point up the significant details (such a
commentary has often to be retrospective), one television
camera can offer a general view of the situation while a second
can pick out the details, the mannerisms, the symptoms that
may be of diagnostic significance. This type of relay we practise
regularly in several psychiatric teaching hospitals – on some
occasions to over two hundred students simultaneously, though
normally the groups are smaller. As with any other medical
teaching use of television, this is never to be considered as a
complete substitute for personal contact with patients; but it is
regarded by the participating psychiatrists as contributing
greatly to the quality of their teaching, and it certainly eases
the ordeal for the patient. One must add the answer to a

question that everyone asks: the patients, almost without exception, are completely undisturbed by the cameras and the cameraman (we do not use remote controls); but their indifference can be at least partly explained by the fact that they are actively engaged in the interview situation and not being asked in any sense to 'perform' or speak direct to the cameras.

The psychiatric interview is perhaps the one that most pressingly demands the sense of privacy which the use of television offers; but we are using the same technique in other medical fields – always, of course, with the patient's knowledge and permission – and in psychology. Our psychologists' present efforts with television are being directed towards building up a library of individual test and interview situations. Here the advantages are numerous. It is valuable, for a start, that the interviewer or tester should have a record of his own performance, so that he can assess it as critically as he would that of a colleague. As in psychiatry, a large eavesdropping audience can be catered for without inhibiting the subject of the test or interview. And there is the very considerable teaching advantage that all the members of a class can simultaneously be introduced to the testing techniques that are involved – in the past this was something that could be achieved with only a small number of students at any one time. Related to this is the further advantage that, with the same subject's performance in a test fully visible and audible to each member of the student audience, it is possible to check whether individual students are all learning to score correctly and on the same basis.

All the work described so far can be undertaken by the cameras in our central pool, although for reasons of convenience we may sometimes use our mobile unit. This unit, planned on the lines we described earlier, took some months to build and it was first put into service in February of 1966. Since then it has developed its own pattern of work, much of it carried on in hospitals throughout the city – though it also travels much farther afield. In subjects like medicine and surgery we have been able to reduce the amount of bedside teaching, to the relief of patient and ward sister alike; and in several medical teaching departments it is now common practice that our unit moves in, sets up in a side-room, and relays the clinical demonstration to a class of students elsewhere. In most cases we also make a recording for subsequent use. In a variety of specialist hospitals – neurosurgical units, orthopaedic wards, limb-fitting centres – we collect and record material for use back in the main lecture rooms of the university. Recordings of this kind are made virtually without rehearsal (other than a broad indication of the consultant's intentions) and without a script; the atmosphere captured is thus that of normal bedside teaching, and we avoid any build-up of tension in the patient.

There is often a shortage of room in the teaching hospitals, and the fact that the whole television control operation can be carried on in the van outside the building is a great help. The unit's flexibility has been further demonstrated by moving into patients' own homes – something a class of students could never do – and compiling case histories on elderly patients for the department of geriatrics. We recorded an account of the home conditions and of the particular domestic difficulties that made hospital treatment necessary. Some weeks later we followed the same patients to hospital, recorded the progress of their treatment, and finally went home with them again to assess its effectiveness. The same sort of mobility has taken us into school classrooms to observe a variety of teaching methods, to a hospital eighty miles away to record an account of their group therapy techniques: and only an outburst of impossible weather conditions frustrated our intention to cover a 'dig' on which our archaeology department was recently engaged.

Implicit in this outline of our activities is the fact that we use videotape extensively, and indeed the effectiveness of our service depends very largely on this use of recording. Its contribution to the work of our mobile unit is obvious; in general it cuts out a lot of repetitive work; and already it has given us a substantial library of medical, psychiatric and psychological material.

There are also situations in which recording makes an even more direct contribution to the acquisition of professional skills. One instance, reminiscent of the 'micro-teaching' idea described in an earlier chapter, is that our final-year divinity students – already accustomed to preaching to each other – now carry out this exercise before the camera as well; and are immediately thereafter subjected not only to the comments of their colleagues but also to the utterly objective assessment afforded by a playback of their own recorded performance. 'On the whole,' says the professor in charge of this activity, 'the traditional methods of instruction in the delivery of sermons have proved frustratingly ineffective. The television method of instruction opens up exciting possibilities.'

Two other educationally valid uses of recording have emerged (most uses are justified by their administrative convenience rather than by any directly educational purpose in the act of recording itself). First, the case of the professor who was disappointed with the quality of seminar work in his Honours class and the sharp distinction between those who were participating and those who were merely passengers. For him we recorded a complete session of the seminar group, playing it back to them some days later. That the results of this playback were effective is suggested by the fact that he presented the same recording, with analytical comment, to the first meeting of his new Honours class at the beginning of the following session. Second, there is the use of recording made by our School of Social Study. There, where students are trained (as prospective social workers of various types) in the principles of effective interviewing and in all aspects of group-control and the group process, our recordings of clinical interviews in social and psychological medicine are used for study and analysis. So, too, are recordings of various types of group work including psychiatric group therapy. 'Irrespective of the content of these interviews,' says the Director of the School, 'the examples already recorded present an impressively wide range of interview techniques, ways of establishing *rapport*, ways of getting quickly to the heart of a case, examples of knowing when and where to stop. I see in these videotapes a big reinforcement of our teaching resources – our tutors will not be confined to the necessarily idiosyncratic material provided by themselves alone.'

Now from all that has been said up to this point, two things will have become clear. We have seldom so far (apart from overflow lectures) presented what one could call complete acts of teaching on television: most of the activities produce items which are incidental, contributory, to a fairly conventional pattern of teaching. We still do not have a studio: yet we have achieved a great deal without it.

The first point is important. It underlines the case for a productive compromise in our thinking about television, for an awareness that television in the university need not be a thing apart, new and revolutionary. Our cameras and traditional teaching methods can meet halfway; and we who provide the television service must be prepared to show as much adaptability as we expect from our colleagues on the teaching side of the partnership. On the second point, to say that we do not have a studio is not absolutely true; for a year ago we stripped a large room down to its barest essentials, hung drapes right around it on curtain rails, and put in as much lighting as some rather elderly wiring would carry. Used in conjunction with our mobile unit, this has provided a very temporary and makeshift studio, and here we have recorded complete lectures and discussion groups, and taken a few of our staff on the first steps towards studio teaching techniques. Meantime our permanent television studio is within sight of completion. It will lie at the centre of a cable distribution system which extends across the whole area of the university, and includes also one of our teaching hospitals. This cable system will, to begin with, offer four channels – that is, four simultaneous transmissions from the studio, or from prerecorded tape, or from film; and, as demand increases, another four channels can be brought into use.

If we claim to have been managing so well without a properly equipped studio, and without a complex distribution system, and if departmental demands did not originally envisage studio-type presentations, why should the need for them now arise? Is this simply one more area in which Parkinson's Law operates? So far as the distribution system is concerned, it makes possible the most economical employment of resources in staff and recording equipment. Until now, we have made recordings on site; and when playback has been required, the videotape machine has once again had to travel – this time to the nominated lecture theatre so that the recording can be played out. Though we shall continue to record many items on site (when the activities cannot reasonably be transferred to a studio), we shall be able to handle transmissions from a central videotape room. This will reduce wear and tear on equipment, cut down on unproductive use of staff time, and eliminate any demand on departmental accommodation or on teaching staff other than the turning of a switch to the appropriate channel.

Of the studio, there is a good deal more to say. One of its uses will undoubtedly be for straight lecturing – or at least the television equivalent of straight lecturing. Already we have done a certain amount of this – in one case, for example, 'banking' a whole series of lectures to cover a period during which the lecturer himself had to be abroad. What, incidentally, is the 'television equivalent' of a straight lecture? To this there are probably many answers; but in our experience some lecturers have found it possible to achieve a much more relaxed and intimate style in their studio lecturing, treating the camera like a group of two or three students, and achieving thereby (if surprisingly) a more intimate contact with their listeners than in the normal classroom situation. There is no reason why the blackboard should be forbidden to the studio lecturer; but – if he is prepared to devote the necessary thought to the matter in advance – we can usually offer him alternatives which are more acceptable. Illustration, by slides or photographic stills or captions, becomes a matter of simplicity; the initial temptation, indeed, may be to over-illustrate simply because the facility is there.

123

Studio lecturing is, of course, the logical solution to the 'overflow' problem. It will not be an attractive proposition to everyone, for many lecturers do genuinely believe themselves to be dependent on the reactions of a class in front of them, and this they can still enjoy if the normal lecture situation is merely being relayed elsewhere. Nevertheless, as we have seen, the overflow method is fundamentally a hybrid and unsatisfactory one; and, if you have gone so far as to accept that half your audience sees you only by television, you may well feel it sensible to decide that all your students should see you in the same way, and that you should come to terms with the medium that makes this possible. Such lecturing may be given live from the studio, but once again recording opens up various administrative possibilities. We are already helping to lighten the burden of repeat-lectures which are needed not because of sheer numbers, but because of syllabus conflicts which demand that exactly the same teaching shall be given to two different groups at different times in the day. This situation we meet by recording the lecture as it is given on the first occasion, and replaying it to the second group; but there is no reason why this procedure should not be multiplied, as time goes on, in ways that will offer a choice of subjects which time-table clashes have in the past made impossible.

Once accept that you may record a lecture and you are faced with the question – does this mean that the same lectures can be churned out from videotape year after year? It does mean just that: the possibility exists. This could be a sensible economy in staff resources, or it could be a devastating threat to our standards of university teaching. But this is not, strictly, a television question; and it is ludicrous to suggest that it is television which creates the threat. Where it is justifiable to re-transmit a lecture, this can be done; where it is not, the tape can be erased. We have all seen lecture notes which are yellow and dog-eared with age; the videotape equivalent is a possibility. For the moment at any rate, one safeguard is that the kind of people who are prepared to use television tend to be the kind who also keep their teaching up to date. The converse, of course, is not to be taken as being true.

However, to return to the studio. One could scarcely justify its provision if it were merely to provide a base for lecturing by television. For this alone, something much simpler would suffice, and something much smaller. The studio will be used for new forms of teaching, and new contributions to the existing forms. Take, for example, the work we have already begun to do for the department of English Literature. The study of pre-scribed texts has often involved analysis of particular passages which have been read to the class by a lecturer: where the pre-scribed text is a play, we have been pre-recording the chosen excerpts – which are subsequently played into the lecture theatre at the appropriate point. Some of these excerpts have been produced very simply in our temporary studio; others have been prepared more elaborately with the assistance of the College of Drama in Glasgow. But the point should be made clear that this is a teaching use of the studio – it is not an exer-cise in drama so much as a direct contribution to the teaching of literature.

It seems likely, however, that the most productive use of the studio will be in the preparation of programmes which could be described as broadly similar to what the broadcasters call documentary. This brings us back to a point originally made in Chapter 2 – that many lectures are arguments based on evi-dence which is referred to, but never produced. It is not pro-duced for the perfectly adequate reason that its production in the normal lecture-room situation would be clumsy, imprac-ticable, and often unintelligible. There will be cases sometimes – and in some departments only – where the evidence can be assembled in our television studio. It may be film clips, or inter-views, or any number of photographic stills, or apparatus, or a group of experts in discussion or it may be all of these together: but the assembly and the orderly presentation of such evidence is one of the main functions of a teaching television studio. Such programmes will not form the daily content of teaching, they

125

will not by any means totally replace the traditional methods; but often they will be seen as a useful way of introducing a course, or summing it up. To us, as television professionals, the encouraging thing is that academic staff who have originally used television in a purely incidental way, or to meet an urgent departmental demand, very frequently begin to see for themselves the tremendous advantages that a studio can offer in the editing, collating, and lucid presentation of the incidental material that we have gathered for them. The studio, in other words, has already justified itself as a necessary third stage in our development as a university television service.

It is perhaps worth our while to look very briefly at two questions which are frequently raised. First, the demands in time which television makes upon teaching staff. Here one comes across some very exaggerated reports, daunting enough to put anyone off the idea of facing the cameras. How much time does television consume? The only honest answer must be that there can be no generalized answer, it all depends on what you are doing with it. If you use television for overflow lecturing, then obviously it takes exactly the same amount of time as ordinary lecturing. If you opt for the logical alternative and give your lecture from a studio, then it may take almost no extra time at all; but if you take advantage of the extra facilities, and want to introduce captions and other illustrative material, then it takes as much extra time as is needed to work out a running order and rough cues for your television director. Depending on how closely and frequently you work with each other, this can be a matter of only a very few minutes. Here, you see, you still have not committed yourself to anything like a closely scripted situation: you are still essentially giving a conventional lecture, but with some illustration that must arrive as you refer to it, or imply a reference to it. This demands liaison, but not a great deal of time.

As you move up the scale, however, towards the fully scripted situation – towards the 'programme' as distinct from the televised lecture – you are faced with quite different circumstances that demand close co-ordination between many people, and precise timing. You must now produce a fully annotated script; everyone must know the precise word at which any particular visual comes up; film and pre-recorded inserts must be cued to the split second. You are now using the full resources of television, and they can consume a great deal of time in rehearsal, and in planning long before you reach that stage. However, the staff of a television service exists to carry much of that load; the more exaggerated estimates of the time consumed by a single programme usually come from people who have unwisely attempted to carry the whole weight, or have been unable to share out the responsibility for graphics, direction, film research, and so on, among staff whose full-time occupations these are.

The other question is about film. Why do we speak so much about the use of videotape for jobs that film could obviously tackle? In general it must be made clear that television and film are not here in competition at all; their uses are complementary, and no television undertaking would go far without incorporating the provision of film. Under certain conditions of lighting, for example, the film camera can cope where television cannot. But for many of our purposes in a university, television and videotape have absolutely clear advantages – no developing and printing stages are involved, your recording is available for immediate replay; an unsuccessful reel of film represents a final loss, and one which you may not discover till some time later, but an unsuccessful tape recording can be immediately checked, erased, and re-shot. The most telling advantage of videotape in much of our work is that it copes so adequately with once-and-for-all situations. To give a polished film account of an activity, you normally shoot, re-shoot, and edit together the most appropriate shots – the activity itself may have to be repeated several times before you collect all the angles and aspects that you require for the final version. With television, you use several cameras simultaneously and 'edit' as you go along, by choosing and recording the shot which at any moment best tells the story.

127

If you are dealing with medical situations, with children, with tests and interviews, with any circumstances in which the chronological veracity of the ultimate recording is vital, the advantages of videotape over film are indisputable.

When we were considering the development of the local education authority systems for schools, it was suggested that there might be possibilities for the exchange of recorded programmes between one city system and another. Does television open the way to the similar exchange of teaching material among the universities? Technically, of course, it certainly does. In theory such exchanges could be carried out live, though this would be an expensive method and would involve substantial time-tabling problems; in practice it is much more likely that material would be sent on videotape from one university to another, provided that the universities concerned had recording machines that were mutually compatible.

The subject areas in which such exchange might be valuable, and the technical means by which they might be brought about, are fully examined in 'University Intercommunication' [18] – a report which was prepared for a working party, drawn from nine universities, which for about three years has been examining the potentiality of links between the teaching faculties of different universities. Television can provide the facilities, but there may be considerable difficulties – of organization and of attitude – to be overcome; and fruitful exchanges will depend not so much on cables and videotapes as on the feelings of academic staff about the value of such exchanges. It may well be that there is a stronger argument for the interchange of case material – as in the medical and psychiatric fields – than of actual recorded teaching; at all events, it is in the related field of psychology that our own earliest exchanges have taken place, with our immediate neighbours in the University of Strathclyde.

CHAPTER TEN

The Teacher and the Producer

A variety of quite natural misgivings afflict the teacher as television moves inward upon our educational institutions, seeming almost to threaten the former privacy of the classroom and the lecture theatre. Some of the misgivings are caused, no doubt, by brief and uninstructed visits to the studios of the professional broadcasters; some by the jargon which, like any foreign language, sounds so much more capable and impressive than our own. First, there is the fear that teaching may come to be dominated by the sheer mechanics of television – whether this means the handling of a single camera in the classroom, or coping with the paraphernalia and the technical talk of the fully-fledged studio. A quite reasonable fear this, which may indeed be well founded. There is at the moment far too much mystique about television: we can get rid of that, but the mechanics cannot be dismissed so lightly. As we have stressed repeatedly, pupils and students these days have grown up with television pictures and techniques that are highly professional, and there is no reason why they should be subjected to amateur standards in the classroom: what is more, they will neither respect nor accept them. Playing about with cameras is an activity guaranteed to produce many hours of innocent enjoyment; but, if you plan to go beyond the simplest visual-aid uses of television

129

then you should consider handing over the technical side of it to someone who is making television his special concern, someone who regards it as his first responsibility to see that the teacher is left free to concentrate on the material of his teaching. Attempt to be master simultaneously of both the teaching and the mechanics, and you will find the mechanics dominating.

Then there is the teacher's fear that the introduction of television will inevitably mean the learning of new techniques: one has heard distressing stories about having to stand on a chalk mark on the floor, and move to another chalk mark at the beginning of the seventh paragraph – or about having to gabble one's way through twenty vital words of introduction in eight seconds precisely, while mysterious things happen to a film insert that comes from somewhere else in the building. Does television mean all this, and is it worth it? Well, there are techniques and tricks that help – without which, in fact, the end-product can only be amateurish and embarrassing; and some of these techniques are absolutely essential when you reach the stage of an elaborate presentation in the studio. None of them are mysterious: once you have shed the frills that belong properly to entertainment television, you are left only with such techniques as are dictated by common sense and the need for planning and efficiency in an operation where many people have to work together, and each must know exactly what all the others are doing. Since studio routines are based on common sense, one finds in practice that members of a teaching staff accept them readily, once the reasons for their existence have been explained.

However, a third, and much more fundamental, fear is that if television makes its way into school systems and universities, then the producer may take over in some senses from the teacher. Built into this fear is the assumption that the teacher and the producer must somehow differ in their aims. E. W. H. Briault, for example, writing about the Inner London closed circuit system, says that educational television 'ought to show teachers teaching by means of television and not producers producing programmes. . . . We require the teacher producer who can retain educational control of programmes' [19]. But merely to produce a new term, to speak of the 'teacher-producer', does not wholly dismiss the problem. Even when we achieve an ideal state of affairs in which teachers have mastered television's techniques, and producers are trained as teachers, even then – in a production situation of any complexity – there will continue to exist the separate functions of teacher and producer. Briefly, and in advance of a fuller explanation of our terms, one can say that in any given programme the teacher will be responsible for the content of the lesson and its delivery to the camera, while the producer will be responsible for its total presentation in television terms.

Now we must pause to consider what we mean by the word 'producer'. In the broadcasting organizations, subject to some local variations, we find two complementary roles filled by two different people who are known as 'producer' and 'director'. It seems not unlikely, by the way, that in the larger closed circuit systems a similar division of responsibilities may emerge. In such a context, the producer is the man who has the over-all control of a programme; he plans its general shape, outlines its theme and sets its tone; he will decide on the main participants, and he will have ultimate control of the budget. The director, on the other hand, is the man who actually puts the show on the air; he is in charge of all the studio activity, he controls the exact placing and movement of the cameras, he makes every on-the-spot decision that is demanded, and the pictures which we see from moment to moment are the pictures of his choice. Now it is often absolutely necessary, in an elaborate programme, that there should be this division of labour; there are frequently occasions, however, on which the choice of shots and the control of cameras is so immediately relevant to the content of a programme – in the case of an unscripted discussion, for example – that the producer may decide to act as director also. For this, or for other reasons, we may find that a programme and the entire studio operation are under the control of only one man. On the whole, this seems to be the most likely pattern in the majority of our educational studios. The one man in charge will combine the functions of both director and producer; and it is in this inclusive sense that we use the word 'producer' in this chapter.

In the simplest sort of educational situation, it is conceivable that producer and teacher are one and the same person; in which case he must within himself strike a balance between the demands of his lesson and of its effective television presentation. Let us assume a basic studio situation, which implies that we have within the studio a teacher-performer, and that we have in the control room another man – whatever his origins – who is acting as producer. The role of the teacher is to provide the content of the lesson. This content will vary in its complexity and in the degree of its preliminary preparation. It may be the off-the-cuff style of interview that a consultant conducts with his patient: it may be a lesson or lecture that is delivered in conventional and partly *ad lib* style, or in a more closely structured studio version: it may be a fully scripted programme wholly designed for television presentation. Whatever the pattern, there is no real ambiguity about the role of the teacher: he is there to provide the central core of teaching material without which all that is going on around him would be utterly pointless activity.

What people are not quite so certain about is the part played by the producer. Is he merely the bellows-boy who pumps air into the organ? Or does he sit at the console, acting – like the organist – as some sort of interpreter between the composer-teacher and his audience? Allowing for all the dangers of any analogy, the producer should for preference be seen in the latter role. What qualifications must the educational producer have, then? What should be his background and experience? What specifically are the areas in which he should have authority?

For a start, he must be trained in the use of the medium, in its principles and practice. He must know the capabilities and the limitations of the equipment he has to handle at the transmission end and, though he will always depend on the advice of his engineering staff, he should be sufficiently acquainted with technical detail to speak to his engineers in their own language and to command their respect. He should have a firm grasp of what goes on at the receiving end too; he should know how viewers react to various types of visual and aural presentation – which means, if you prefer to put it that way, that he must have studied the theories of motivation and perception. He must know what makes a good teaching script. This implies that he must be able to sense the most appropriate distribution of stress and stimulus throughout the programme (a responsibility which is of course fully shared by the teacher); and that he clearly appreciates the principles which distinguish our spoken language from the written forms (to which academics all too readily commit themselves the moment they put pen to paper). Many of these and other related skills the good producer has acquired almost instinctively; but a groundwork of practical training is indispensable before one can come to terms with the pure mechanics of studio procedure. And though in the early days of educational television it may be the most convenient arrangement to import producers who have learned their craft in the sphere of broadcasting, there is no reason why the schools and universities should not be able quite soon to secure for their teaching staff the practical experience and training that will qualify them to act as producers. Although their functions in the studio may differ, the characteristic qualities which make the good producer and the good teacher overlap to a considerable degree.

To return to the responsibilities of the producer as such: he is, above all else, an organizer and co-ordinator. He it is who must create a coherent relationship between all the elements in the construction of a programme. He must pull together, edit, and adjust the first rough script which the teacher presents to him. He must in general terms supervise the production of graphics material, ensuring that captions and diagrams and photographic stills will make their point in relation to the spoken content of the lesson. He must decide which of the available resources can most appropriately be employed – is this a job for film, for animated caption, or would a quick montage of photographs do the job with equal effect and greater economy? The producer will arrange for any research that is necessary, the examination of library film, the checking of copyrights if this arises. He will search for the appropriate music and sound effects. For all these organizational details he must take the general responsibility; and, when the time for transmission or recording comes around, he has the final supervision of all the sound and vision that leaves the studio.

All this would be true of the producer in any context. In educational television, it is reasonable to expect that he should also have a sound knowledge of learning theory. This is a knowledge which, when he is working with trained teachers, he will presumably share with his performers. But it has to be pointed out, with some diffidence, that in the case of university teachers – for such is our system – he may often be working with performers who have never in fact made any formal study of the learning processes: they are expert in their subject rather than its presentation. This means first, that it is all the more important for the producer to be himself a teacher by training; and second, that tact must be one of his stronger qualities.

The broadcast producer, whatever field he works in – whether it be light entertainment or current affairs or drama or religion – must be capable of identifying himself with the representative viewer. In the absence of that immediate audience reaction which can be so useful a guide to the speaker or artiste of any kind, he must be able to use his own judgment as to the audience which he believes himself to be addressing, and the material he presents to them. In educational television, the producer has a similar role: he must, in one part of his mind, become the pupil or the student. From that he must move on to exercise the most difficult, yet the most vital, part of his function – he must become the performer's constructive but absolutely objective critic. In the discharge of his duty as critic, the producer provides a valuable element that is normally completely absent

from the teaching situation. Obviously this could in unfavour
able circumstances be regarded as an intrusion; but many a
teacher will find that the communication of his ideas to a third
party during the preparation of a programme, coupled with
well-instructed criticism during rehearsal, has the effect of
clarifying his own thoughts about his subject and sharpening
the outline of his argument.

Now we come to the crux of the matter. In broadcasting,
the producer offers his criticism and it is accepted – with or
without a good grace. The producer, to all intents and purposes, hires and fires; and even if that ultimate sanction were
never to be a conscious consideration, he is by accepted conven-
tion the man in charge. But who, in the educational situation,
is the man in charge? – is it the producer, or the teacher? Just
at the moment, if this were ever to become a really acute issue,
it might present itself as a tussle between two different professional backgrounds; because in these early days, as we know, the
producer and the teacher tend to represent respectively purely
broadcasting and purely teaching experience. Before long it can
be expected that television skills will be grafted on to the
educationist, and a new type of educational specialist will
emerge. Even then, as between two types both wholly within the
teaching profession, the question of priorities will arise, though
it may be variously expressed. Some will ask 'Who is in charge –
the teacher or the producer?': others will say 'Which matters
more – the teaching content or the television presentation?'

To present the question in terms of conflict is, however, to
over-dramatize the issue. That there will be sincere differences of
opinion from time to time is inevitable; but on the whole it is a
matter of balance – and the balance will swing this way or that
according to the precise form of educational television in which
we are for any one period engaged. And here we come right
back to the thesis from which we started long ago: we must
differentiate quite clearly between the various uses of television.
If your use of television is that of a distribution system intended
primarily for direct teaching (as in the case of the local authority

systems) the balance will tip firmly towards the teacher. This does not mean that the producer and his skills are to be dispensed with: he must still exercise his knowledge of what makes for clear and intelligible communication. But the first call on his professional skill will now be the provision of whatever makes for the best teaching relevant to all the prevailing circumstances.

You may, however, be using television still within the educational setting but much more strictly *as* television – using it, that is, because of the peculiar techniques and facilities which it offers, but with a teaching purpose. One thinks, for example, of the complex studio presentation which derives its impact from the skilful fusion of many different resources; or of the techniques involved in shaping a meaningful account of classroom observation. In such cases the balance between teacher and producer will be very evenly held: say rather, that the professional skills of teaching and of television will be equally indispensable. But come full circle, and move back into the world of broadcasting: the educator may still want to use television as a mass medium, as the crossbreed offspring of showbusiness and journalism which it sometimes is. In that case, the balance inevitably swings back towards the producer, the television professional; the educator must be prepared to accept the compromise in style and in intellectual approach which this decision may imply.

The strictly neutral mechanics of television can be used in an infinite variety of ways, in many directions and at many levels. The level and direction of our educational television, the width of the beam we want to project, these are questions which in any one context must be decided as matters of policy. If the policy is clear, the balances of authority within the television team will sort themselves out accordingly.

Appendix

A NEW DEVELOPMENT – EVR

The Preface to this book suggested that it is rash to offer firm predictions about educational television at a time when developments are so rapid. And sure enough, since the main chapters were completed we have been given notice of yet another technical development which is due to be presented for our inspection in Britain some time in the spring of 1968, and should be generally available to us by 1969 or 1970. This development is known as EVR – electronic video recording and reproduction – and the now almost routine claim is made that it will 'revolutionize the world of educational television'. The use of quotation marks is meant to imply not that the claim is unjustified, but merely that it must be examined.

First, then, a brief description of the system. Detailed technical accounts of EVR have, understandably, not been released; but the process is one by which both sound and vision from existing film or videotape material are transferred to unperforated film, which reaches the user in small cartridges or cassettes – their actual size is seven inches in diameter, and half an inch thick. Though these cassettes contain film, it is through a television set that the programme is viewed – the cassette being inserted into a special player which is attached to the set. EVR will initially be available in monochrome, but colour will follow.

Without going into the economics of the system at the moment, EVR has a number of obvious practical advantages. For one thing, its use for reproduction does not depend (as videotape does) on one's owning a videotape recorder. An ordinary television set, the special player attachment, and the film cartridge are all that one needs. The size of the cartridge

K

compares very favourably with the spool of videotape – in round terms, a given amount of programme material on EVR film occupies just one hundredth of the sheer bulk involved in an equivalent professional videotape recording: and this could be quite an important consideration if one were thinking of regular exchanges of recordings between educational institutions. There is every reason to expect that the system will offer a standard of reproduction appreciably higher than that which we associate with the projection of 8-mm or 16-mm film; and it is even claimed that the actual process of transfer to EVR offers opportunities of improving on the original recording – though it would be prudent to suppose that such improvement must amount to nothing more than a 'sharpening up' of the image.

What about costs? Naturally, these are meantime quoted in somewhat provisional terms; but the playback device – the special attachment to one's television set – is likely to cost around £80 to £100. The cassettes – that is, the film which contains the programme material – will probably cost about £10 for one hour's playing time; and each film should have a life of at least 500 reproductions. It is reasonable to suppose, however, that the actual sale price of the films will be affected substantially by the source of the original recordings and the various rights that may be held in their content.

One other figure – again a provisional one – should be quoted at this point. To have a videotape of your own (for example, a recording prepared by a school or university television service) transferred to an EVR master copy would cost something like £100 per hour of programme – this, of course, is a figure that takes no account of any special payments to performers, payment for copyright, etc.: it is simply the cost of translation from videotape or film on to a master copy of the special film which goes into the EVR cartridge.

One further point. Those responsible for launching the EVR project regard themselves, initially at any rate, as providing simply a processing facility. In other words, they do not meantime plan to produce original educational programmes: they hope to draw on material already created and produced by existing educational agencies, giving it wider circulation and the possibility of more flexible use because of the simple reproduction facilities that their system offers.

How is this development likely to affect the pattern of educational television, when it becomes generally available to us? First, one must stress that there are wide areas of the work described in this book which will simply not be affected by EVR. All the 'live' uses of television for magnification, distribution, and relay in its various forms, must remain essentially live and essentially local functions. And all those uses of television (broadcast or closed circuit) which depend for their impact on immediacy of time will be unaffected. But, as we have seen, only a small proportion of educational television does depend on immediacy of time: most of the teaching television which has been structured into programmes is as valid tomorrow as it is today, and (other things being equal) would be as acceptable from an EVR cartridge as from a spool of videotape.

Secondly, we should note that EVR does not in itself imply any changes in production technique or style of presentation: these will continue to be determined by the needs of the audience aimed at, and by the factors which already condition the preparation of any material which is to be viewed on a television monitor. So an EVR film cartridge may dispense everything from the broadest of enrichment teaching to the most directly didactic. Economic and commercial considerations, however, are among those which will determine what type of material actually does find its way into the EVR cassettes. How great is the demand likely to be for EVR, or for any similar systems which may emerge? In which sectors of educational television, as we currently know it, is the cassette likely to replace existing forms of distribution, supplement them, or find an entirely new market?

Schools broadcasting, by the BBC and independent companies, seems unlikely to be directly affected. Its capacity for nation-wide and simultaneous distribution, the sheer simplicity with which it can be received on an ordinary set in the classroom, and the fact that it is to all intents and purposes available 'free', leave it in the very strongest of positions. On the other hand, one shortcoming of the schools broadcast has always been the difficulty of fitting it into a local time-table pattern. This can nowadays be overcome, in the case of sound radio, by recording off transmission and using the recording at a time more suitable to the individual school. It is not yet permissible to do the same with television programmes: and, even if it were, how many individual schools will be able to afford the videotape recorder with which to do it? Because the standards of equipment available (and the relevant prices) are changing so rapidly these days, exact costs have not been quoted throughout the preceding chapters; in the course of a few months they might become quite misleading. But at this point in time, early in 1968, one can offer these very general comparisons – that the cost of the very cheapest videotape recorder available for the individual school would be around five times as much as the expected cost of an EVR player; that the cost of videotape for such a machine and the cost of EVR cartridges would just about break even, with the balance slightly in favour of EVR; that the quality of EVR recordings and reproductions should be very much higher than that available on cheap videotape machines; *but* that a videotape can be erased and used repeatedly for other recordings, whereas outlay on EVR film (as on any other film) is final.

However, such comparisons based on the individual school are probably rather artificial. If the EVR idea catches on, it is surely much more likely that a cassette copy of an originally broadcast programme would be bought to serve a number of schools – and it is obviously a more economic proposition to equip every school with an EVR player than it is to give every school a VTR. Briefly, then: EVR could overcome the difficulty of fitting broadcast television programmes into the school time-table – always assuming that the broadcasters agree to such copying of their material: on the basis of both cost and quality, such a system seems preferable to local video-recording off broadcast transmission (which is not meantime permissible in any case).

But if an individual school really wants and needs a programme, one still wonders whether it would not be both cheaper and more reasonable to adjust its time-table than to resort to either the EVR or the videotape alternative.

Turn now to the area closed circuit systems like those in Glasgow, Hull, London, Plymouth. On a technical point, one should explain that the EVR cassette – although envisaged primarily as operating with one television set – could equally be used to feed programmes through a closed circuit system; and occasions may well arise when the cassette is so used, just as film is often used nowadays. But our main consideration at the moment is to ask whether the arrival of EVR will in any substantial way supplant the local systems which have grown up. Such systems would still appear, when compared with EVR, to have all the advantages claimed for them in Chapter 6 – local relevance and appeal, considerable flexibility in time-tabling, possibility of rapid feed-back, and so on. But such networks are only likely to exist in large city areas: and, in the closing pages of Chapter 6, attention was drawn to the fact that the county and rural areas lying outside the big cities have needs which are just as urgent, but which for economic reasons cannot be met by extended cable systems. Here is a field in which EVR might well make a most significant contribution – distributing by cassette those kinds of teaching which Glasgow and London and the others have found it practicable to distribute by cable. Obviously one would calculate costs on the basis of circulating programme cassettes around a number of schools. Obviously, too, such a system would be subject to exactly the same difficulties as are experienced in the rapid and efficient circulation of films. But if, in the rural areas, there is a genuine demand for the kind of specialist teaching now being given by television in a few big cities, then EVR does seem to offer realistic possibilities. One major production centre could thus serve a much larger area than it can meantime reach by its own distribution system.

Having said this, there are one or two cautionary notes which may as well be interjected here as anywhere. EVR depends on an original film or videotape production – that is to say, it takes care of distribution in its own way; but somewhere or other you still need the television or film facilities to make your programme: you must have your own studio, or – directly or indirectly – pay someone else for the use of theirs. So the £100 which (at a provisional estimate) it costs to copy an hour's material on to an EVR master film is a figure which must be added to original production costs, however these may be shared out. And the figure of £10 or thereabouts, which is quoted as the likely cost of an hour-long cassette available for general purchase, is a figure based on the forecast that it will only be economic to produce 200 or more cassettes of any one programme.

If this seems confusing, it may help to point out that two quite separate possibilities should emerge, to meet two different types of demand. One, that EVR will as a commercial proposition make and market copies of existing programmes (for the sake of argument, let us say a popular BBC schools series) – programmes of which they are reasonably certain to sell upwards of 200 copies: such programmes will be available to the purchaser at about £10 per hour's material. The second and separate possibility follows a pattern like this: local authority A, which has its own closed circuit system, has made a series of direct-teaching programmes using scarce specialist teachers: local authority B has no closed circuit system, but does have school television sets fitted with EVR players, so it uses EVR's processing facility to have master copies made of A's series, and this costs something like £100 an hour – for the master copy. Multiple copies required for distribution throughout B's area will cost less, the exact figure being determined not by commercial considerations but by processing costs and by the financial arrangements arrived at between local authorities A and B. And of course other permutations are possible: for example, programmes originally designed and produced by the ILEA closed circuit system, and proved successful there, could be copied and marketed commercially. All this, it must be clearly understood, is speculation about possibilities – not a statement of policies expressed by any of the bodies hypothetically referred to.

Regarded as a system operating within Britain alone – and it is in this country that it is first to be launched – EVR may not have so large a potential for intra-mural teaching in the universities. We have, after all, a total of 44 universities at the moment; and, even if we take the substantially larger figure which would include other institutions offering higher education, we must still remember 200 as the number of copies at which commercial distribution breaks even. As for the direct inter-university exchanges of television material which may develop, it seems likely that videotape machines will soon be fairly generally held in the universities, and one would hope that their mutual compatibility will be ensured; so small-scale exchanges on videotape could operate quite satisfactorily. Failing that, an original videotape copied to 16-mm film can certainly be reproduced in any university or college: it may be a long time before one can be equally certain about facilities for reproducing the film specially made for EVR.

But if we turn from the conventional university situation to the completely new possibilities that are opened up by the prospect of an Open University, where does EVR or any similar system fit in? One element in the Open University's teaching – it is only one element, and has been given disproportionate publicity – will be the provision of television programmes. Until now, the only obvious possibilities have been either to use spare time on an existing channel or to set up a new channel explicitly for the University. To both these possibilities theoretical objections of varying strength and validity have been advanced: for example – that one channel could not possibly carry all the programmes which an Open University should want to offer; that broadcast programmes (particularly if restricted to one channel) could not be scheduled so flexibly as to meet the viewing hours of all potential students; that broadcast channels should in any case be used for the broad mass of the public which pays for them, not for the specialized requirements of a very small minority. Without going into the rights and wrongs of these arguments here, one can see how largely they might be met if it should prove practicable to use a system like EVR as a supplement to broadcast transmissions of Open University teaching. In the home, in small tutorial groups, or on any local closed circuit system existing primarily for some other purpose, programmes could be viewed at the times most suitable for the individual or group concerned. Meantime the demands on broadcast channel time could be held at a reasonable level. Programme cassettes could presumably be circulated to enrolled students, as individuals or in groups: but here, as elsewhere, economic considerations will prove a decisive factor, and these will need very detailed study.

With some diffidence then, for the accuracy of these speculations will be proved or disproved very shortly, one would suggest that EVR (or similar systems which one must expect may develop) is most likely to be of value in three main educational fields. These are – the secondary distribution of schools programmes already broadcast; the provision for schools in outlying areas of those types of service which the big-city closed circuit systems are already providing over their own networks; and the distribution (probably as a supplement to broadcasting) of the television element in Open University teaching. To these three probabilities one should perhaps add one more – that, for professional refresher courses of the kind referred to at page 52, courses for people 'scattered one here, two there – forming a sizable group, but one ill-suited to the conventional idea of gathering in adult classes,' EVR may well be the answer. This will not be one of the earlier developments, since the cost of the EVR player will discourage its installation in the home so long as only educational programmes are available for it. However the EVR project, once launched successfully in the educational field, may be expected to extend into the entertainment field as well. When that happens, and a mass audience is catered for, one of the welcome side effects could be the provision of a much wider range of minority-appeal cultural and educational material as well.

References

1 *Broadcasting:* Memorandum on the Report of the Committee on Broadcasting, 1960 (published by HMSO, Cmnd. 1770, July 1962)

2 ITV 1963, p. 100 (published by Independent Television Authority)

3 *Teaching through Television* by Harold Wiltshire and Fred Bayliss (published by National Institute of Adult Education and University of Nottingham)

4 *Correspondence Teaching and Television* by H. D. Perraton (published by National Extension College, 1966)

5 *Scottish Television Medical Programmes* by A. Elliot Bell and Gavin Shaw (Scottish Medical Journal, 1966, 11: 250)

6 BBC Press release dated 31 October 1935

7 BBC Handbook 1959, p. 109

8 BBC Handbook 1962, p. 78

9 *Television Teaching Today* by Henry R. Cassirer, p. 238 (published by Unesco, 1960)

10 BBC School Television Broadcasting, a Report on the First Two Years (published by BBC, 1959)

11 Paper by Signora Puglisi, delivered to Council of Europe Seminar on Direct Teaching by Television, Rome, 1966

12 *Educational Television and Radio in Britain*, p. 102 (published by BBC, 1966)

13 ibid., p. 111

14 ibid., p. 115

15 *The Warblington Experiment in Closed Circuit Television* (published by County Education Officer for Hampshire, 1965)

16 *CETO News*, No. 6, March 1965 (published by Centre for Educational Television Overseas)

17 *Audio-Visual Aids in Higher Scientific Education* (published by HMSO, 1965)
18 *University Intercommunication – the Nine Universities Research Project* (published by Pergamon Press, 1966)
19 *Educational Television and Radio in Britain*, p. 115

Bibliography

Audio-Visual Aids in Higher Scientific Education
the report of the Brynmor Jones Committee, published by HMSO, 1965

A Guide to Instructional Television
by Robert M. Diamond, published McGraw-Hill Book Co. Ltd, New York, 1964

A University of the Air
A White Paper, published by HMSO, 1966, Cmnd. 2922

British Broadcasting in Transition
by B. Paulu, published by Macmillan, London, 1961

Broadcasting and the Community
by J. Scupham, published by C. A. Watts, London, 1967

Closed Circuit Television in Education in Great Britain
Experimental Development Unit Report No. 2, published by National Committee for Audio-Visual Aids in Education, 33 Queen Anne Street, London, W.1, 1965

Educational Television and Radio in Britain
papers prepared for a conference organized by the BBC and the University of Sussex, published by BBC, 1966

Educational Television Guidebook
by Philip Lewis, published McGraw-Hill Book Co., New York, 1961

English Language Teaching and Television
by S. Pit Corder, published Longmans, 1960

146

Mass Communication in Britain
  by R. Hoggart, in *The Modern Age*, ed. B. Ford, published by
  Pelican Books, Harmondsworth, 1961
*Problems of Television Research: a Progress Report of the Tele-
  vision Research Committee*
  by J. D. Halloran, published by Leicester University Press,
  1966
*Report of the Committee on Broadcasting, 1960 (The Pilkington
  Report)*
  published by HMSO, 1962, Cmnd. 1753
*Report of the Committee on University Teaching Methods (The
  Hale Report)*
  published by HMSO, 1964
School Broadcasting and the Newsom Report
  a lecture by John Scupham, published by BBC, 1965
Teaching Through Television
  a report on teaching Science by television in schools, published by OECD, 1960, and available through HMSO
Techniques of Television Production
  by Rudy Bretz, published by McGraw-Hill, New York, 1960
*Television and the Child: An Empirical Study of the Effect of
  Television on the Young,*
  by H. T. Himmelweit, A. N. Oppenheim and P. Vince,
  published by Oxford University Press, 1958
Television for Schools
  a lecture by Kenneth Fawdry, published by BBC, 1967
Television in the University
  report of a Granada Seminar on CCTV in the Universities,
  published by Granada TV Ltd, and distributed by Mac-
  Gibbon and Kee Ltd, 1965
Television Teaching Today
  a Unesco report by Henry R. Cassirer, published by Unesco
  and available through HMSO, 1960
*The Effects of Mass Communication with Special Reference to
  Television*
  by J. D. Halloran, published by Leicester University Press,
  1965

Television in Education

The Grammar of TV Production
   by D. Davis, published Barrie and Rockliffe, 1960

The Uses of Literacy
   by R. Hoggart, published by Penguin Books, Harmondsworth, 1958

Understanding Media
   by Marshall McLuhan, published by Routledge and Kegan Paul, 1964

Index

149